AN ADAPTED CLASSIC

Things Fall Apart

Chinua Achebe

Upper Saddle River, New Jersey
www.globefearon.com

This Globe Fearon adapted edition is published by permission of Heinemann Educational Publishers, a division of Reed Educational and Professional Publishing Limited © 1958.

Adapter: Sandra Widner
Project Editor: Kevin Iwano
Senior Editor: Lynn Kloss
Production Editor: Travis Bailey
Marketing Manager: Kate Krimsky
Art Supervision: Sharon Ferguson
Electronic Page Production: Mimi Raihl, Lissette Quiñones
Cover and Interior Illustrator: Suling Wang

Printed in the United States of America
2 3 4 5 6 7 8 9 10 04 03 02 01

ISBN 0-130-23501-6

CONTENTS

ABOUT THE AUTHOR

Chinua Achebe (CHEE noo ah Ah CHAY bay) is celebrated for "defining a modern African literature that was truly African," according to the London *Sunday Times*. He is the best-known and most influential African writer of his generation.

Achebe was born in the Ibo (now spelled Igbo) village of Ogidi, in eastern Nigeria. He is the fifth child of an instructor in Christian studies. During Achebe's childhood, Nigeria was a British colony. As a member of an educated, English-speaking family, Achebe grew up in a privileged position.

He graduated from the University College in Ibadan in Nigeria in 1953. Then he became a radio producer. Three years later, on a trip to London to attend the British Broadcasting Corporation's Staff School, Achebe submitted *Things Fall Apart* to a publisher. The novel was published in 1958; it was an instant success.

Achebe returned to Nigeria to work at the Nigerian Broadcasting Corporation, although he continued to write. As a director, he focused on developing a national identity for Nigeria. Then, in 1966, Nigeria began years of political unrest. Igbo officers overthrew the government, which was overthrown again by non-Igbo soldiers. Achebe fled. He worked at the University of Nigeria at a campus away from the government. He also began lecturing overseas.

From 1972–1976 and 1987–1988, Achebe was a professor of English at the University of Massachusetts, and then at the University of Connecticut. Today, he lives in New York with his wife, where they both teach at Bard College. Achebe has received many awards for his work.

ADAPTER'S NOTE

In preparing this edition of *Things Fall Apart,* we have kept as close as possible to Chinua Achebe's original words and style. We have shortened some chapters. The footnotes explain Igbo words and some other difficult words. A glossary of Igbo words is in the back of the book.

PREFACE

Things Fall Apart has been translated into 45 languages and has sold millions of copies. Many consider this the most famous novel about Africa.

Some African writers have argued that their culture can only be understood if they write in their native language. Achebe views his use of English as a way of introducing his land and its culture to a world that would otherwise pay no attention.

The book's title is taken from a stanza of a poem called "The Second Coming" by the poet W. B. Yeats:

Turning and turning in the widening gyre
The falcon cannot hear the falconer;
Things fall apart; the center cannot hold,
Mere anarchy is loosed upon the world.

This poem describes a world breaking down. The novel shows customs and beliefs breaking down in a traditional African society.

Achebe has said that one reason he wrote this book was to explain a complex African society to a world that thinks of it as simple and primitive.

In *Things Fall Apart,* Achebe succeeds in showing a complicated, rich world. He has created characters readers can both understand and identify with.

HISTORICAL BACKGROUND

Nigeria is just north of the Equator and south of the Sahara Desert. There are more than 200 ethnic groups living there. The three largest groups are the Yoruba in the west, the Igbo in the east, and the Hausa-Fulani in the north.

The Igbo are ancient inhabitants of the land. Their ancestors lived in Africa at least 10,000 years ago. Until the late 19th century, the Igbo lived in small communities. There was little contact with the outside world. However, the British had begun to colonize Africa a century earlier.

The events of this novel take place at the turn of the 20th century. As other European powers began to move into West Africa, the British declared Nigeria their colony.

British rule was heavy-handed. An entire village could be punished for the crimes of one person. Opposition to British rule resulted in the deaths of many Igbo.

The British created a class of Nigerians who were educated in Britain. Eventually, this group helped demand freedom from colonial rule. In 1960, Nigeria became independent.

CULTURAL NOTES

Things Fall Apart describes a society with complex laws and customs. The Igbo have a government and an artistic tradition. They have a judicial system, a religion, and a monetary system.

The Igbo society described in this book is based on a tradition of laws and behavior passed from generation to generation. The Igbo use stories, proverbs, and folktales to pass on these traditions. At night, parents and their children tell stories. These tales pass on the wisdom and tradition of the tribe. Because this is an oral society, those who are accomplished speakers are revered.

Igbo society is organized in clans, and within clans, villages. Men run society. A man may have as many wives as he can afford, and the children of his wives belong to him. When a man decides to marry, he offers money (bride-price) to his fiancée's family.

The number of wives a man has is one way to tell his wealth. Other ways are the number of yams he has and the number of titles he has taken in the clan. There are four titles. Each is more expensive than the last. Only a few men in any generation are able to afford all four titles in the clan.

Achebe points out that in this society, a man's family history is less important than what he is able to accomplish. This tribe respects achievement more than family history. Some in the society are outcasts, however. The *osu,* claimed by the gods, are shunned by society and must be buried in the Evil Forest, where evil spirits are said to live.

Igbo society is based on farming. A man's worth is determined in part by how good a farmer of yams he is. Yams are considered a man's crop; women grow other crops, such as cassava (a root) and maize (corn). Men clear the forest and then burn the field. As land becomes worn out, farmers move farther from the village to clear new land.

The religion of the Igbo is based on a series of gods and ancestral spirits who decide, through priests, what the people must do. These gods require offerings and obedience. A group of respected and wealthy men serve as *egwugwu,* who are said to embody the ancestral spirits of the tribe.

Many of these Igbo traditions are still practiced today. Igbo oral tradition is practiced to pass on the social, religious, and educational beliefs to younger generations. Passing on these beliefs has helped to preserve the unique Igbo traditions.

MAJOR CHARACTERS

Agbala (AG ba la) The Oracle of the Hills and Caves; he is the messenger of Ani; he is served by a priestess; Agbala is a male although his name also can mean "woman"

Chielo (CHEE eh loh) Priestess of Agbala and best friend of Ekwefi

Ekwefi (eh KWEH fee) Okonkwo's second wife; mother of Ezinma and of nine other children who died when young

Ezinma (eh ZEEN mah) Ekwefi's child; a favorite of Okonkwo

Ikemefuna (ee keh MEH foo nah) A boy given to Umuofia to avoid war; he is lively and clever

Nwoye (nuh-WHO-yeh) Okonkwo's son; a sensitive young man considered weak by his father

Obierika (oh bee AIR ee kah) Okonkwo's best friend; father of Maduka

Ojiubo (oh jee OOH boh) Okonkwo's third wife

Okonkwo (oh KAWN kwo) The main character of the book; he is a driven man who is a successful farmer and warrior who has tried his entire life to overcome the legacy of his lazy father

Mr. Brown First white missionary in Umuofia; he is understanding and helpful

Mr. Smith Mr. Brown's successor who is hard and unyielding in his attitude toward the Igbo

Unoka (ooh NO kah) Okonkwo's father who is considered lazy and weak by his society and his son

Part 1 Okonkwo and His Clan

Chapter 1

Okonkwo was well known throughout the nine villages and even beyond. His fame rested on solid achievements. As a young man of eighteen, he had brought honor to his village. He had thrown the great wrestler named Amalinze the Cat, who for seven years was unbeaten. The old men agreed it was one of the fiercest fights ever.

The drums beat and the spectators held their breath. Amalinze knew how to fight, but Okonkwo was as slippery as a fish in water. Every nerve and muscle stood out on their arms and on their backs. In the end, Okonkwo threw the Cat.

That was twenty years ago or more. During this time, Okonkwo's fame had grown. He was tall and huge, and his bushy eyebrows and wide nose gave him a very severe look. When he walked, he seemed to walk on springs, as if he was going to pounce. And he did pounce on people quite often. He had a slight stammer, and when he was angry and could not get his words out quickly enough, he used his fists. He had no patience with unsuccessful men. He had no patience with his father.

Unoka, Okonkwo's father, had died ten years ago. In his day, Unoka had been lazy and quite incapable of thinking about tomorrow. If any money came his way, and it seldom did, he immediately called round his neighbors and made merry. Unoka was, of course, a debtor, and he owed every neighbor some money.

Unoka was tall but very thin and had a slight stoop. He looked haggard and mournful except when he was drinking or playing his flute. He was very good on his flute, and his happiest moments were the times after the harvest when he played with the village musicians.

Unoka was poor and his wife and children had barely enough to eat. People laughed at him because he was a loafer, and they swore never to lend him any more money because he never paid them back.

One day a neighbor called Okoye came to see him. Unoka was playing his flute. He shook hands with Okoye, who unrolled the goatskin he carried under his arm, and sat down. Unoka went to an inner room and returned with a small wooden disc containing a kola nut,[1] alligator pepper, and a lump of white chalk.

"I have kola," Unoka announced.

"Thank you. He who brings kola brings life. But I think you ought to break it," replied Okoye, passing back the disc. Finally, Unoka accepted the honor of breaking the kola. Okoye took the lump of chalk, drew lines on the floor, and painted his big toe.

As he broke the kola, Unoka prayed for life and health and protection against enemies. The two men spoke of many things: the heavy rains, a coming war with a nearby village. Unoka was never happy when it came to wars. He was in fact a coward and could not bear the sight of blood. And so he changed the subject and talked about music, and his face beamed.

Okoye was also a musician. But he was not a failure like Unoka. He had a large barn full of yams, and he had three wives. Now he was going to take a title, the third highest in the land. It was a very expensive ceremony and he was gathering all his resources.

---

1. kola nut a nut inside the kola; it is sectional like a grapefruit

That was why he had come to see Unoka. He cleared his throat and began:

"Thank you for the kola. You may have heard of the title I intend to take shortly."

Having spoken plainly so far, Okoye said the next half a dozen sentences in proverbs. Among the Igbo, the art of conversation is revered. Finally, Okoye hit the subject. He wanted Unoka to return the two hundred cowries Unoka had borrowed two years ago. As soon as he understood, Unoka burst out laughing. He laughed loud and long and tears stood in his eyes. His visitor was amazed and sat speechless.

"Look at that wall," Unoka finally said between outbursts of laughter. He pointed to the far wall of his hut. It was rubbed with red earth so it shone. "Look at those lines of chalk." There were five groups, and the smallest group had ten lines. Unoka continued: "Each group there represents a debt to someone, and each stroke is one hundred cowries. You see, I owe that man a thousand cowries. I shall pay you, but not today. I shall pay my big debts first." Okoye left.

When Unoka died, he had taken no title at all and was heavily in debt. Was it any wonder then that his son Okonkwo was ashamed of him? Fortunately, among these people a man was judged according to his worth, not the worth of his father.

Okonkwo was clearly cut out for great things. He was still young but he had won fame as the greatest wrestler in the nine villages. He was a wealthy farmer and had two barns full of yams, and he had just married his third wife. To crown it all, he had taken two titles and had shown great bravery in two wars. Although Okonkwo was young, he was already one of the greatest men of his time. Age was respected among his people, but achievement was revered. That was how he came to look after the doomed lad Ikemefuna who was sacrificed to Umuofia[2] to avoid war.

Chapter 2

Okonkwo had just blown out the palm-oil lamp and stretched himself on his bamboo bed when he heard the gong of the town crier piercing the still night air. *Gome, gome, gome, gome,* boomed the hollow metal. Then the crier gave his message, and at the end of it beat his instrument again. This was the message: Every man of Umuofia was asked to gather at the marketplace tomorrow morning. Okonkwo wondered what was wrong. He had heard a clear overtone of tragedy in the crier's voice.

Okonkwo on his bamboo bed tried to figure out the nature of the emergency—war with a neighboring clan? That seemed the most likely reason for the message, and he was not afraid of war. He was a man of war. Unlike his father, Okonkwo could stand the look of blood.

In the morning, the marketplace was full. There must have been about ten thousand men there, all talking in low voices. At last Ogbuefi Ezeugo stood up in the midst of them and bellowed four times, "*Umuofia kwenu,*" a greeting to the men in the market place. Ten thousand men answered. "*Yaa!*" each time. Then there was perfect silence. Ogbuefi Ezeugo was a powerful orator and was always chosen to speak on such occasions. He moved his hand over his white head and stroked his white beard.

---

2. Umuofia a group of nine villages that formed Okonkwo's clan

"Umuofia kwenu," he bellowed a fifth time, and the crowd yelled in answer. Then suddenly, like one possessed, he shot out his left hand and pointed in the direction of Mbaino. Through gleaming white teeth firmly clenched, he said: "Those sons of wild animals have dared to murder a daughter of Umuofia." He threw his head down and gnashed his teeth. When he began again, the anger on his face was gone. In its place a sort of smile hovered, more terrible than the anger. In an unemotional voice, he told Umuofia how their daughter had gone to market at Mbaino and had been killed. That woman, said Ezeugo, was the wife of Ogbuefi Udo, and he pointed to a man who sat near him with a bowed head. The crowd then shouted with anger.

Many others spoke, and at the end it was decided to follow the normal course of action. An ultimatum was immediately dispatched to Mbaino asking the people to choose between war and the offer of a young man and a virgin as compensation.[3]

Umuofia was feared by all its neighbors. The village was powerful in war and magic. The neighboring clans would not go to war against Umuofia without first trying a peaceful settlement. In fairness to Umuofia, it should be recorded that the village never went to war unless its case was just and was accepted as such by its Oracle—the Oracle of the Hills and the Caves. There were indeed times when the Oracle had forbidden Umuofia to wage war. If the clan had disobeyed, the people would surely have been beaten.

But the war that now threatened was a just war. Even the enemy clan knew that. And so when Okonkwo of Umuofia arrived at Mbaino as the proud

---

3. compensation payment

emissary[4] of war, he was treated with great respect. Two days later, he returned home with a lad of fifteen and a young virgin. The lad's name was Ikemefuna, whose sad story is still told in Umuofia today.

The elders met to hear a report of Okonkwo's mission. At the end they decided, as everybody knew they would, that the girl should go to Ogbuefi Udo to replace his murdered wife. The boy belonged to the clan as a whole, and there was no hurry to decide his fate. Okonkwo was asked on behalf of the clan to look after him. And so for three years Ikemefuna lived in Okonkwo's household.

Okonkwo ruled his household with a heavy hand. His wives lived in fear of his fiery temper and so did his little children. Perhaps in his heart Okonkwo was not a cruel man. But his whole life was dominated by the fear of failure and of weakness. It was deeper than the fear of evil gods or the forces of nature. Okonkwo's fear was of himself: lest he should be found to resemble his father. Even as a little boy he had resented his father's failure, and he remembered how he had suffered when a playmate had told him his father was *agbala*.[5] That was how Okonkwo came to know that *agbala* did not only mean "woman," it could also mean a man who had taken no title. And so Okonkwo was ruled by one passion—to hate everything his father Unoka had loved. One of those things was gentleness, and another was idleness.

During the planting season, Okonkwo worked daily on his farms from sunup to sundown. He was a very strong man and rarely felt tired. But his wives

---

4. emissary person sent on a mission

5. *agbala* woman; also used to refer to a man with no title

and young children were not as strong, and so they suffered. However, they dared not complain openly. Okonkwo's first son, Nwoye, was then twelve years old but was already causing his father great anxiety for his laziness. At any rate, that was how it looked to his father, and Okonkwo sought to correct Nwoye by constant nagging and discipline. And so Nwoye was developing into a sad-faced youth.

Okonkwo's prosperity was visible. He had a large compound enclosed by a thick wall of red earth. His own hut stood behind the only gate in the red walls. Each of his three wives had her own hut, which together formed a half moon behind his hut. The barn was built against one end of the red walls. Long stacks of yams stood out prosperously in it. At the opposite end of the compound was a shed for the goats, and each wife built a small attachment to her hut for the hens. Near the barn was a small house, the shrine where Okonkwo kept the wooden symbols of his personal god and of his ancestral spirits. He worshipped them with sacrifices of kola nut, food, and palm-wine, and offered prayer to them on behalf of himself, his three wives, and his eight children.

So when the daughter of Umuofia was killed in Mbaino, the boy Ikemefuna came into Okonkwo's household. Okonkwo called his most senior wife.

"He belongs to the clan," Okonkwo told her. "Look after him."

"Is he staying long with us?" she asked.

"Do what you are told," Okonkwo thundered.

And so Nwoye's mother took Ikemefuna to her hut and asked no more questions.

Ikemefuna was terribly afraid. He could not understand what was happening to him. How could he know that his father had taken a hand in killing a daughter of Umuofia? All he knew was that a few men had arrived at his house, talking with his father in low tones. Then he had been taken out and handed to a stranger. His mother had wept bitterly. And so the stranger had brought him and a girl a long way from home.

Chapter 3

Okonkwo did not have the start in life that many young men had. He did not inherit a barn from his father. There was no barn to inherit. The story was told of how his father, Unoka, had gone to consult the Oracle of the Hills and the Caves to find out why he always had a miserable harvest.

People came from far and near to consult the Oracle, who was called Agbala. They came when misfortune occurred, or to discover their future.

The way into the shrine was a small round hole at the side of a hill. Worshippers and those who came to seek knowledge from the god crawled on their belly through the hole and found themselves in a dark space in the presence of Agbala. No one had ever beheld him, except his priestess, who stood by the sacred fire, which she built in the heart of the cave.

When Okonkwo was a boy, his father had gone to consult Agbala. The priestess then was a woman called Chika. She was full of the power of her god, and she was greatly feared. Unoka began his story.

"Every year," he said sadly, "before I put any crop in the ground, I make a sacrifice to Ani, the owner of all land. I clear the bush and set fire to it when it is dry. I sow the yams when the rain has fallen, and stake them when young plants appear. I weed—"

"Hold your peace!" screamed the priestess, her voice terrible. "You have offended neither the gods nor your fathers. And when a man is at peace with his gods and his ancestors, his harvest will be good or bad according to the strength of his arm. You, Unoka, are known in all the clan for the weakness of your hoe. When your neighbors clear forests, you sow on tired farms that take no labor to clear. They cross seven rivers to make their farms; you stay home and offer sacrifices. Go home and work like a man."

Unoka was ill-fated. He had a bad *chi,*[6] and evil fortune followed him to his death. He died of the swelling that was hateful to the earth goddess. A man with this swelling in his stomach and limbs was carried to the Evil Forest and left there to die. The sickness was a horror to the earth, and so the victim could not be buried in the earth. He died and rotted away above the earth and was not given a burial. Such was Unoka's fate. When they carried him away, he took his flute.

Okonkwo neither inherited a barn nor a title, nor even a young wife. In spite of this, he began even in his father's lifetime to lay the foundations of a prosperous future. It was slow and painful, but he threw himself into it like one possessed. Indeed he was possessed by the fear of his father's shameful life and death.

There was a wealthy man in Okonkwo's village who had three huge barns, nine wives, and thirty children.

---

6. *chi* personal god

It was for this man, Nwakibie, that Okonkwo worked to earn his first seed yams.

Okonkwo took a pot of palm-wine and a cock to Nwakibie. Two elderly neighbors were sent for, and Nwakibie's two grown-up sons were also present in his hut. Okonkwo presented a kola nut and an alligator pepper, which were passed around. He broke the nut, saying, "We pray for life, for children, for a good harvest and for happiness. You will have what is good for you and I will have what is good for me."

After the kola had been eaten, Okonkwo brought his palm-wine and stood it in the center of the group.

"I have brought you this little kola," he said to Nwakibie. "As our people say, a man who pays respect to the great paves the way for his own greatness. I have come to pay you my respects and also to ask a favor. But let us drink the wine first."

Everybody thanked Okonkwo. The first cup went to Okonkwo, who must taste his wine first. The group drank, beginning with the eldest man. Then Nwakibie sent for his wives. Only four came in.

"Is Anasi not in?" he asked. Anasi was the first wife and the others could not drink before her. Then Anasi came. She was middle-aged, tall, and strongly built. She looked every inch the ruler of the women in a large and prosperous family. She wore the anklet of her husband's titles, which only the first wife could wear.

Anasi accepted the horn from her husband, went down on one knee, drank a little, and handed back the horn. She rose and went back to her hut. The other wives drank the same way and went away.

The men continued drinking and talking. They were discussing the palm-wine tapper, who suddenly gave up his trade.

"Obiako has always been a strange one," said Nwakibie. "I have heard that many years ago, when his father had not been dead very long, he had gone to consult the Oracle. The Oracle told him, 'Your dead father wants you to sacrifice a goat to him.' He told the Oracle, 'Ask my dead father if he ever had a fowl when he was alive.' " Everyone laughed heartily except Okonkwo, who laughed uneasily. As the saying goes, an old woman is always uneasy when dry bones are mentioned in a proverb. Okonkwo remembered his own father.

After the wine had been drunk, Okonkwo laid his difficulties before Nwakibie.

"I have come to you for help," he said. "I have cleared a farm but have no yams. I know what it is to ask a man to trust another with his yams. I am not afraid of work. If you give me some yam seeds, I will not fail you."

Nwakibie cleared his throat. "It pleases me to see a young man like you when our youth has gone so soft. Many young men have come to me for yams, but I have refused. But I can trust you. I know it as I look at you. As our fathers said, you can tell a ripe corn by its look. I shall give you twice four hundred yams. Go ahead and prepare your farm."

Okonkwo thanked him and went home happy. He had not hoped to get more than four hundred seeds. He would have to make a bigger farm.

Share-cropping[7] was a very slow way of building up a barn of one's own. After all the toil, one only got a third of the harvest. But for Okonkwo, there was no other way. What made it worse was that Okonkwo was also supporting his mother, his sisters, and his father, because his mother could not be expected to

---

7. share-cropping giving a landlord a share of the crops raised instead of rent money

eat while her husband starved. His mother and sisters worked hard enough, but they grew women's crops, like coco-yams, beans, and cassava. Yam was a man's crop.

The year Okonkwo took eight hundred seed yams from Nwakibie was the worst year in memory. It seemed as if the world had gone mad. The first rains were late, and, when they came, they lasted only a brief moment. The blazing sun returned and scorched all the green that had appeared. Like all good farmers, Okonkwo had begun to sow with the first rains. He had already sown four hundred seeds when the rains dried up and the heat returned. The drought continued for eight weeks and the yams were killed.

Okonkwo planted what he had left of his seed-yams when the rains finally returned. He had one consolation. The yams he had sown before the drought were his own. He still had the eight hundred from Nwakibie and four hundred from a friend of his father. So he would make a fresh start.

But that year had gone mad. Now the rain fell as it had never fallen before. It poured down violently and washed away the yams. The harvest that year was sad, like a funeral, and many farmers wept as they dug up the miserable and rotting yams.

Okonkwo remembered that tragic year with a cold shiver throughout the rest of his life. He knew that he was a fierce fighter, but that year had been enough to break the heart of a lion.

"I survived that year," he always said, "so I will survive anything."

His father Unoka, who was then an ailing man, had said to him during the terrible harvest, "I know you will not despair. You have a manly and a proud heart. A proud heart can survive a general failure because such a failure does not prick its pride."

Unoka was like that in his last days. His love of talk had grown with age and sickness. It tried Okonkwo's patience beyond words.

Chapter 4

Okonkwo had risen from poverty to be one of the lords of the clan. The old man bore him no ill will. Indeed, he respected him for his hard work. But he was struck, as most people were, by Okonkwo's scorn for less successful men. A week ago, a man had contradicted Okonkwo at a meeting held to discuss the next feast. Without looking at the man Okonkwo had said, "This meeting is for men." The man who had contradicted him had no titles. That was why Okonkwo had called him a woman. Okonkwo knew how to kill a man's spirit.

Everybody at the meeting took sides with Osugo when Okonkwo called him a woman. The oldest man present said sternly that those whose palm-kernels were cracked for them by a benevolent[8] spirit should not forget to be humble. Okonkwo said he was sorry, and the meeting continued.

But it was really not true that Okonkwo's palm-kernels had been cracked for him. He had cracked them himself. Anyone who knew his grim struggle against poverty could not say he had just been lucky. If ever a man deserved his success, that man was Okonkwo. His fame at wrestling was not luck. At the most, one could say that his *chi,* or personal god, was good.

---

8. benevolent kind or generous

But the Igbo people have a proverb that when a man says yes his *chi* says yes also. Okonkwo said yes very strongly, and his *chi* agreed. His clan agreed, too, because it judged a man by his work. That was why Okonkwo had been chosen by his clan to carry a message of war to their enemies unless they agreed to give up a young man and a virgin as compensation for the killing of Udo's wife.

The elders of the clan had decided that Ikemefuna should be in Okonkwo's care for a while. But no one thought it would be for three years. They seemed to forget Ikemefuna as soon as they had taken the decision.

At first, Ikemefuna was very afraid. Once or twice he tried to run away, but he did not know where to begin. He thought of his mother and his three-year-old sister, and he wept bitterly. Nwoye's mother was very kind to him, but all he said was, "When shall I go home?" When Okonkwo heard Ikemefuna would not eat, he came into the hut with a big stick and stood over Ikemefuna while he ate his yams. A few moments later, Ikemefuna went behind the hut and vomited. Nwoye's mother went to him and placed her hands on his chest. Ikemefuna was ill for three weeks, and when he recovered, he seemed to have overcome his great fear and sadness.

He was by nature a lively boy, and he became popular in Okonkwo's household. Okonkwo's son Nwoye, who was two years younger, became inseparable from him. Ikemefuna seemed to know everything. He could make flutes from bamboo stems. He knew the names of all the birds. He knew which trees made the strongest bows.

Even Okonkwo became fond of the boy—inwardly of course. Okonkwo never showed any emotion openly except anger. He thought that to show affection was a sign of weakness; the only thing worth demonstrating was strength. He therefore treated Ikemefuna as he treated everybody—with a heavy hand. But there was no doubt he liked the boy. Sometimes when Okonkwo went to meetings he allowed Ikemefuna to come with him, like a son, carrying his stool and his goatskin bag. Indeed, Ikemefuna called him father.

Ikemefuna came to Umuofia at the end of the carefree season between harvest and planting. That was also the year Okonkwo broke the peace and was punished by Ezeani, the priest of the earth goddess.

Okonkwo was provoked to anger by his youngest wife, who went to braid her hair at her friend's house and did not return in time to cook the afternoon meal. After waiting in vain for her dish, he went to her hut to see what she was doing. There was nobody in the hut and the fireplace was cold.

"Where is Ojiugo?" he asked his second wife.

"She has gone to braid her hair."

"Where are her children? Did she take them?" he asked with unusual restraint.

"They are here," his first wife, Nwoye's mother said. Okonkwo bent down and looked into her hut. Ojiugo's children were eating.

"Did she ask you to feed them before she went?"

"Yes," lied Nwoye's mother.

Okonkwo knew she was lying. When Ojiugo returned, he beat her heavily. In his anger, he had forgotten that it was the Week of Peace. His first two wives ran out in alarm, pleading with him that it was the sacred week. But Okonkwo was not one to stop beating someone, not even for fear of a goddess.

Okonkwo's neighbors heard his wife crying and asked over the walls what was the matter. It was unheard of to beat somebody during the sacred week.

Before dusk, Ezeani, priest of the earth goddess Ani, called on Okonkwo. Okonkwo brought out a kola nut.

"Take away your kola nut. I shall not eat in the house of a man who has no respect for our gods."

Okonkwo tried to explain what his wife had done. Ezeani paid no attention. "Listen to me," he said. "You know that our forefathers said that before we plant crops, we should observe a week in which a man does not say a harsh word. You have committed a great evil." He brought down his staff heavily. "The evil you have done can ruin the whole clan." His tone changed from anger to command. "You will bring to the shrine of Ani tomorrow one she-goat, one hen, a length of cloth, and a hundred cowries." He rose and left the hut.

Okonkwo did as the priest said. Inwardly, he was sorry, but he was not the man to tell his neighbors he was in error. And so people said he had no respect for the gods of the clan.

No work was done during the Week of Peace. People called on their neighbors. This year they talked of nothing but what Okonkwo had done. It was the first time for many years that a man had broken the sacred peace.

After the Week of Peace, every man and his family began to clear the bush to make new farms. The cut bush was left to dry and fire was then set to it. Okonkwo spent the next few days preparing his seed-yams. Sometimes he decided a yam was too big, and split it along its length. His eldest son, Nwoye, and Ikemefuna helped in fetching the yams and in counting the prepared seeds. Sometimes Okonkwo gave them a few yams to prepare. But he always found fault with their effort.

"If you split another yam of this size, I shall break your jaw. And you," he said to Ikemefuna, "do you not grow yams where you come from?"

Inwardly, Okonkwo knew the boys were still too young to understand the difficult art of preparing seed-yams. But he thought one could not begin too early. Yams stood for manliness, and he who could feed his family was a great man. Okonkwo wanted his son to be a great man. He would stamp out the signs of laziness he thought he already saw in him.

Some days later, after two or three heavy rains, Okonkwo and his family went to the farm with baskets of seed-yams and their hoes and machetes, and they began the planting. They made mounds of earth in straight lines and sowed the yams in them.

Yam, the king of crops, was a demanding king. For three or four moons, it required hard work and constant attention. The young stems were protected from heat with rings of sword-shaped leaves. As the rains became heavier, the women planted maize, melons, and beans between the yam mounds. The yams were then staked. The women weeded the farm at three specific times.

Now the rains had really come. Sometimes it poured down in such thick sheets that earth and sky seemed merged. At such times, in each of the thatched huts of Umuofia, children sat around their mother's cooking fire telling stories, or with their father in his hut, warming themselves from a log fire, roasting, and eating maize. It was a brief resting period between the demanding planting season and the equally exacting but lighthearted month of harvests.

Ikemefuna had begun to feel like a member of Okonkwo's family. He still thought of his mother and his sister, and he had moments of sadness. But he and Nwoye had become deeply attached. Ikemefuna had an endless stock of folktales. Nwoye remembered this period vividly until the end of his life. He even remembered how he had laughed when Ikemefuna had told him that the proper name for a corn cob with only a few scattered grains was "teeth of an old woman."

Gradually the rain became lighter and less frequent, and earth and sky once again became separate. Children no longer stayed indoors but ran about singing.

Chapter 5

The Feast of the New Yam was approaching and Umuofia was in a festive mood. It was time for giving thanks to Ani, the earth goddess.

The Feast of the New Yam was held every year before the harvest. New yams could not be eaten until some had first been offered to the earth goddess and the ancestral spirits of the clan. Everyone looked forward to the New Yam Festival because it began the season of plenty. On the last night before the festival, old yams were disposed of. The new year must begin with tasty, fresh yams. All cooking pots and bowls were washed, especially the wooden mortar, or bowl, in which yam was pounded. Yam *foo-foo*[9] and vegetable soup were the chief foods of the celebration. There was always a large quantity of food left over.

---

9. *foo-foo* a dough made from mashed yams

Every man whose arm was strong, as the Igbo people say, was expected to invite large numbers of guests. Okonkwo always asked his wives' relations, and since he now had three wives, his guests would make a fairly large crowd.

Okonkwo was never as enthusiastic over feasts as most people. He was uncomfortable sitting around. He was much happier working on his farm.

The festival was now three days away. Okonkwo's wives had scrubbed the walls and the huts with red earth until they reflected light. They had drawn patterns on them in white, yellow, and dark green. Then they painted themselves with cam wood and drew beautiful black patterns on their stomachs and their backs. The children were also decorated, especially their hair, which was shaved in patterns.

Then the storm burst. Okonkwo, who had been walking around aimlessly in suppressed[10] anger, found an outlet.

"Who killed this banana tree?" he said.

A hush fell on the compound immediately.

As a matter of fact, the tree was very much alive. Okonkwo's second wife had merely cut a few leaves to wrap some food, and she said this to Okonkwo. Without further argument, Okonkwo gave her a sound beating and left her and her only daughter weeping.

His anger thus satisfied, Okonkwo decided to go hunting. He had an old rusty gun. But although Okonkwo was a great man, he was not a hunter. In fact, he had never killed with his gun. When he called Ikemefuna to fetch it, the wife who had just been beaten murmured about guns that never shot. Unfortunately for her, Okonkwo heard it and ran madly into his room for the loaded gun, ran out and aimed at her as she climbed over the wall.

---

10. suppressed concealed

He pressed the trigger, and there was a loud noise. He threw down the gun and jumped over the wall. There lay the woman, shaken and frightened but unhurt. He heaved a heavy sigh and went away with the gun.

In spite of this incident, the festival was celebrated with great joy in Okonkwo's household. Okonkwo offered a sacrifice of new yam and palm-oil to his ancestors and asked them to protect him, his children, and their mothers in the new year.

As the day wore on his in-laws arrived, each with a huge pot of palm-wine. There was eating and drinking until all the guests left for their homes.

The second day of the new year was the day of the great wrestling match between Okonkwo's village and their neighbors. It was difficult to say which the people enjoyed more—the feasting on the first day or the wrestling contest on the second. One woman had no doubt. She was Okonkwo's second wife, Ekwefi, whom he nearly shot. There was no festival that gave her as much pleasure as the wrestling match. Many years ago when she was the village beauty, Okonkwo had won her heart by throwing the Cat. She did not marry him then, for he was too poor to pay her bride-price. But a few years later she ran away from her husband and came to live with Okonkwo. Now Ekwefi was a woman of forty-five who had suffered a great deal. However, her love of wrestling was as strong as it had been thirty years ago.

The distant beating of drums began to reach them. It came from the direction of the village playground where all the great ceremonies and dances took place. The drums beat the unmistakable wrestling dance—quick and light, the sound came floating on the wind.

Okonkwo cleared his throat and moved his feet to the beat of the drums. It filled him with fire as it had always done. He trembled with the desire to conquer.

"We shall be late for the wrestling," said Ezinma to her mother.

"The drums begin at noon but the wrestling waits until the sun begins to sink. See if your father has brought out yams for the afternoon."

"He has. Nwoye's mother is already cooking."

"Go and bring our own, then. We must cook quickly or we shall be late for the wrestling."

Ezinma peeled the yams quickly. She cut them into small pieces and began to prepare a stew, also using some chicken.

At that moment they heard someone weeping. It sounded like Obiageli, Nwoye's sister.

"Is that not Obiageli weeping?" Ekwefi called across the yard.

"Yes," said Nwoye's mother. "She must have broken her waterpot."

The children filed in, carrying on their heads pots of various sizes suitable to their years. Obiageli brought up the rear, her face streaming with tears.

"What happened?" her mother asked, and Obiageli told the mournful story. Her mother promised to buy her another pot.

Nwoye's younger brothers were about to tell their mother the true story when Ikemefuna looked at them sternly. The fact was that Obiageli had been showing off, balancing the pot on her head with her arms folded in front of her. When the pot fell and broke, she burst out laughing. She only began to weep when they neared the compound.

The drums were still beating. Their sound was no longer separate from the village. It was like the pulsation of its heart. It throbbed in the air, in the sunshine, and even in the trees, and filled the village with excitement.

Ekwefi ladled her husband's share of the stew into a bowl. Ezinma took it to him in his hut.

Okonkwo was sitting on a goatskin already eating his first wife's meal. Obiageli, who had brought it from her mother's hut, sat on the floor waiting for him to finish. Ezinma placed her mother's dish before him and sat with Obiageli.

"Father, will you go to see the wrestling?" Ezinma asked.

"Yes," he answered. "Will you go?"

"Yes." And after a pause she said, "Can I bring your chair for you?"

"No, that is a boy's job." Okonkwo was especially fond of Ezinma. She looked very much like her mother, who was once the village beauty. But his fondness only showed on very rare occasions.

He uncovered his second wife's dish and began to eat from it. Obiageli took the first dish and returned to her mother's hut. Then Nkechi came in, bringing the third dish. Nkechi was the daughter of Okonkwo's third wife.

In the distance the drums continued to beat.

Chapter 6

The whole village turned out, men, women, and children. They stood in a huge circle leaving the center of the village green free. The elders sat on their own stools brought by their young sons or slaves. Okonkwo was among them. All others stood except those who came early enough to secure places on the few stands that had been built.

The drummers sat in front of the huge circle of spectators, facing the elders. Behind them was the ancient, sacred silk-cotton tree. Spirits of good children lived in that tree waiting to be born.

There were seven drums arranged in size in a long wooden basket. Three men beat them with sticks, working from one drum to another. They were possessed by the spirit of the drums.

The young men who kept order on these occasions dashed about. Once in a while, two of them carrying palm fronds[11] ran around the circle and kept the crowd back by beating the ground in front of them.

At last the two teams of wrestlers danced into the circle and the crowd roared and clapped. The drums rose to a frenzy. The people surged forward. Old men nodded to the beat of the drums and remembered the days when they wrestled to its rhythm.

The contest began with boys of fifteen or sixteen, three to a team. They were not the real wrestlers; they merely set the scene. Soon the first two bouts were over. The third created a big sensation even among the elders who did not usually show their excitement. It was as quick as the other two, perhaps quicker. But very few people had seen that kind of wrestling before. One of the wrestlers did something no one could describe because it had been quick as a flash. And the other boy was flat on his back. The crowd roared. Okonkwo sprang to his feet and quickly sat down again. Three young men from the winning team ran forward, carried the boy shoulder high, and danced through the cheering crowd. Everybody soon knew the boy was Maduka, the son of Obierika.

---

11. fronds palm leaves

The drummers stopped briefly before the real matches. Their bodies shone with sweat. They drank water and ate kola nuts, and became ordinary people again, talking and laughing. The air, which had been stretched tight with excitement, relaxed. People looked around and saw those who stood next to them.

"I did not know it was you," Ekwefi said to the woman next to her.

"I do not blame you," said the woman. "I have never seen such a large crowd. Is it true Okonkwo nearly killed you with his gun?"

"It is indeed true, my dear friend. I cannot yet find a mouth with which to tell the story."

"Your *chi* is very much awake, my friend. And how is my daughter, Ezinma?"

"She has been very well for some time now."

"How old is she now?"

"She is about ten years old."

The woman with whom she talked was called Chielo. She was the priestess of Agbala, the Oracle of the Hills and the Caves. In ordinary life, Chielo was a widow with two children. She was very friendly with Ekwefi and they shared a shed in the market. She was particularly fond of Ekwefi's only daughter, Ezinma, whom she called "my daughter." Anyone seeing Chielo in ordinary life would hardly believe she was the same person who prophesied when the spirit of Agbala was upon her.

The contest continued. The two teams faced each other. A young man from one team danced across the center and pointed at whomever he wanted to fight.

There were twelve men and the challenge went from one side to the other. Two judges walked around the wrestlers and stopped them when the fighters were equally matched. Five matches ended this way. But the really exciting moments were when a man was thrown. The huge voice of the crowd then rose to the sky.

The last match was between the leaders of the teams. They were among the best wrestlers in all the nine villages. Some said Okafo was the better man; others said he was not the equal of Ikezue. Last year neither had thrown the other.

Dusk was beginning when their contest began. It was a fierce contest. Ikezue strove to pitch Okafo backwards, but each one knew what the other was thinking.

The wrestlers were now almost still in each other's grip. Their muscles stood out and twitched. It looked like an equal match. Then Ikezue, now desperate, went down quickly on one knee in an attempt to fling his man backwards over his head. It was a sad miscalculation. Quick as lightning, Okafo raised his right leg and swung it over his rival's head. The crowd burst into a thunderous roar. Okafo was swept off his feet and carried home shoulder high. They sang his praise and young women clapped their hands.

Chapter 7

For three years, Ikemefuna lived in Okonkwo's household and the elders of Umuofia seemed to have forgotten about him. He was like an elder brother to Nwoye and seemed to have kindled a new fire in the younger boy. He made him feel grown-up, and they no longer spent the evenings in mother's hut but now sat with Okonkwo in his hut. Nothing pleased Nwoye now more than to be sent for by his mother to do one of those difficult and masculine tasks such as splitting wood or pounding food. On receiving such a message, Nwoye would pretend to be annoyed and grumble aloud about women and their troubles.

Okonkwo was inwardly pleased at his son's development, and he knew it was because of Ikemefuna. Okonkwo wanted Nwoye to grow into a tough young man. He wanted him to be prosperous, with enough food in his barn to feed the ancestors with sacrifices. And so Okonkwo was always happy when he heard Nwoye grumbling about women. That showed in time he would be able to control his women-folk. No matter how prosperous a man was, if he was unable to rule his women and children, he was not really a man.

Okonkwo encouraged the boys to sit with him, and he told them masculine stories of violence and bloodshed. Nwoye knew it was right to be violent, but he still preferred the stories his mother used to tell—stories of the tortoise and his wily[12] ways and of the bird who challenged the world to a wrestling contest. He remembered the story of the quarrel between Earth and Sky. When Nwoye's mother sang this song, he felt carried to distant scenes.

These were the stories Nwoye loved. But he now knew they were for foolish women and children, and he knew his father wanted him to be a man. So he pretended he no longer cared for women's stories. He could see his father was pleased because Okonkwo no longer beat him. So Nwoye and Ikemefuna would listen to Okonkwo's stories of tribal wars. As he told them of the past, they sat in darkness or the dim glow of logs, waiting for the women to finish cooking.

---

12. wily crafty

When they finished, each brought her bowl of *foo-foo* and bowl of soup to her husband. An oil lamp was lit and Okonkwo tasted from each bowl, and then he passed two shares to Nwoye and Ikemefuna.

In this way, moons and seasons passed. Then the locusts came. It had not happened for many a year. The elders said the locusts came once in a generation. They came in the cold season after the harvests had been gathered and ate up all the wild grass. Then, the elders said, they went back to their caves in a distant land where they were guarded by a race of stunted men.

Okonkwo and the two boys were working on the red outer walls of the compound. This was one of the lighter tasks of the after-harvest season. A new cover of thick palm leaves was set on the walls to protect them from the next rainy season.

The women had gone to the bush to collect firewood; the little children had gone to visit their playmates in other compounds. Okonkwo and the boys worked in silence, which was broken only when a new frond was lifted onto the wall or when a busy hen moved dry leaves about in her search for food.

Then quite suddenly, a shadow fell on the world. Okonkwo looked up and wondered if it was going to rain at such an unlikely time of year. But almost immediately a shout of joy broke out.

"Locusts are descending!" was joyfully chanted everywhere, and men, women, and children left their work or their play and ran into the open to see the unfamiliar sight. The locusts had not come for many years, and only the old people had seen them before.

At first, a fairly small swarm came. Then appeared a slowly moving mass like a boundless sheet of black cloud. Soon it covered half the sky. It was a tremendous sight of power and beauty.

Everyone was now about, talking excitedly and praying that the locusts should camp in Umuofia for the night. Although the locusts had not visited for many years, everybody knew they were very good to eat. At last the locusts did descend. They settled on the roofs and covered the ground. Mighty tree branches broke under them, and the country became the brown color of the vast swarm.

Many people went out with baskets trying to catch them, but the elders counseled patience until nightfall. And they were right. The locusts settled in the bushes and their wings became wet with dew. Then everyone filled bags and pots with locusts. The next morning they were roasted in clay pots and spread in the sun until they became dry. For many days, this rare food was eaten with palm-oil.

Okonkwo sat in his hut crunching happily with Ikemefuna and Nwoye and drinking palm-wine, when Ogbuefi Ezeudu came in. Ezeudu was the oldest man in this part of Umuofia. He had been a great and fearless warrior, and he was now accorded great respect. He refused to join the meal, and he asked Onkonkwo to have a word with him outside. When they were out of earshot, he said to Okonkwo:

"That boy calls you father. Do not bear a hand in his death. Yes, Umuofia has decided to kill him. The Oracle of the Hills and Caves has pronounced it. They will take him outside Umuofia as is the custom and kill him there. But I want you to have nothing to do with it because he calls you his father."

The next day, a group of elders from all the nine villages of Umuofia came to Okonkwo's house early in the morning. Nwoye and Ikemefuna were sent out. The elders did not stay long, but when they went away, Okonkwo sat still for a long time. Later that day, he called Ikemefuna and told him he was to be taken home the next day. Nwoye overheard and burst into tears, whereupon his father beat him heavily. As for Ikemefuna, he was at a loss. His own home had gradually become faint and distant. He still missed his mother and sister, but somehow he knew he was not going to see them. He remembered when men had talked in low tones with his father, and now it seemed it was happening all over again.

Later, Nwoye went to his mother's hut and told her that Ikemefuna was going home. She folded her arms and sighed, "Poor child."

The next day, the men returned with a pot of wine. They were all dressed as if they were going to a big clan meeting. Okonkwo got ready quickly and the party set out with Ikemefuna carrying the pot of wine. A deathly silence descended on Okonkwo's compound. Even the very little children seemed to know. Throughout that day, Nwoye sat in his mother's hut and tears filled his eyes.

At the beginning of the journey, the men of Umuofia laughed about the locusts and their women. But as they left Umuofia, silence fell upon them too.

The footway had become a narrow line in the heart of the forest. The undergrowth gave way to giant trees untouched by the ax and the bush-fire. The sun threw a pattern of light and shade on the footway.

Thus the men of Umuofia pursued their way, armed with sheathed[13] machetes, and Ikemefuna, carrying a pot of palm-wine on his head, walked in their midst. He was not afraid now. Okonkwo walked behind him. He could hardly imagine that Okonkwo was not his real father. He had never been fond of his real father. But his mother and three-year-old sister. . . of course, she would be six now. Would he

---

13. sheathed covered

recognize her now? She must have grown quite big. How his mother would weep for joy and thank Okonkwo for having looked after him so well. He would tell her about Nwoye and his mother, and about the locusts. . . . Then quite suddenly, a thought came upon him. His mother might be dead. He tried in vain to force the thought out of his mind. Then he tried to settle the matter by singing a song and walking to its beat. If the song ended on his right foot, his mother was alive. If it ended on his left, she was dead.

One of the men behind him cleared his throat. Ikemefuna looked back, and the man growled at him to go on. The way he said it sent cold fear down Ikemefuna's back. His hands trembled vaguely on the black pot he carried. Why had Okonkwo withdrawn to the rear? Ikemefuna felt his legs melting under him. He was afraid to look back.

As the man who had cleared his throat drew up and raised his machete, Okonkwo looked away. He heard the blow. The pot fell and broke in the sand. He heard Ikemefuna cry, "My father, they have killed me!" as he ran toward him. Dazed with fear, Okonkwo drew his machete and cut Ikemefuna down. He was afraid of being thought weak.

As soon as his father walked in, Nwoye knew that Ikemefuna had been killed, and something seemed to give way inside him, like the snapping of a tightened bow. He did not cry. He just hung limp. He had had the same kind of feeling not long ago, during the last harvest season. Every child loved the harvest season. If they could not help digging up the yams, they could gather firewood for roasting the ones that would be eaten there on the farm.

It was after such a day that Nwoye had felt for the first time a snapping inside him like the one he now felt. They were returning home when they heard the voice of an infant crying in the thick forest. A sudden hush had fallen over the women, who had been talking, and they quickened their steps. Nwoye had heard that twins were put in earthenware pots and thrown away in the forest, but he had never come across them. A vague chill had descended on him. Then something had given way inside him. It came on him again, this feeling, when his father walked in, that night after killing Ikemefuna.

Chapter 8

Okonkwo did not taste any food for two days after the death of Ikemefuna. He drank palm-wine from morning till night, and his eyes were red and fierce like the eyes of a rat when it was caught by the tail and dashed against the floor. He called his son, Nwoye, to sit with him. But the boy was afraid of him and slipped out as soon as he saw Okonkwo dozing.

Okonkwo did not sleep at night. He tried not to think about Ikemefuna, but the more he tried the more he thought about him. Now and then a cold shiver spread down his body.

On the third day, he asked his second wife, Ekwefi, to roast plantains for him. She prepared them the way he liked—with slices of oil-bean and fish.

"You have not eaten for two days," said his daughter Ezinma when she brought the food. "So you must finish this." She sat down. Okonkwo ate the food absentmindedly. She should have been a boy, he thought. He passed her a piece of fish.

"Go and bring me some cold water," he said. Ezinma soon returned with a bowl of cool water from the earthen pot in her mother's hut. Okonkwo took the bowl from her and gulped the water. He ate a few more pieces of plantain and pushed the dish aside.

Ezinma went back to her mother's hut. "She should have been a boy," Okonkwo said to himself again. His mind went back to Ikemefuna, and he shivered. If only he could find some work to do he could forget, but it was the season of rest.

"When did you become a shivering old woman," Okonkwo asked himself, "you, who are known in all the nine villages for your courage in war? How can a man who has killed five men in battle fall to pieces because he has added a boy to their number?"

He sprang to his feet and went to visit his friend Obierika. Obierika was sitting outside making thatches from leaves of the raffia-palm. He led the way into his hut.

"I was coming over to see you as soon as I finished that thatch," he said.

"Is it well?" Okonkwo asked.

"Yes," replied Obierika. "My daughter's suitor is coming today and I hope we will settle the matter of the bride-price. I want you to be there."

Just then Obierika's son, Maduka, came into the hut and greeted Okonkwo.

"Come and shake hands with me," Okonkwo said to the lad. "Your wrestling the other day gave me much happiness." The boy smiled, shook hands with Okonkwo and went into the compound.

"He will do great things," Okonkwo said. "If I had a son like him, I should be happy. I am worried about Nwoye. A bowl of yams can throw him in a wrestling match. His two younger brothers are more promising. I can tell you, Obierika, that my children do not resemble me. If Ezinma had been a boy, I would have been happier. She has the right spirit."

"You worry yourself for nothing," said Obierika. "The children are still very young."

"At Nwoye's age, I was already fending for myself. No, my friend, he is not too young. I have done my best to make Nwoye grow into a man, but there is too much of his mother in him."

"Too much of his grandfather," Obierika thought, but he did not say it. The same thought also came to Okonkwo's mind. But whenever the thought of his father's failure troubled him, he expelled it by thinking about his own success. And so he did now. His mind went to his latest show of manliness.

"I cannot understand why you refused to come with us to kill that boy," he said to Obierika.

"Because I did not want to," Obierika said sharply.

"You sound as if you question the authority and the decision of the Oracle, who said he should die."

"I do not. Why should I? But the Oracle did not ask me to carry out its decision."

"But someone had to do it. If we were all afraid of blood, it would not be done."

"You know very well, Okonkwo, that I am not afraid of blood, and if anyone tells you that I am, he is telling a lie. And let me tell you one thing, my friend. If I were you, I would have stayed home. What you have done will not please the Earth. It is the kind of action for which the goddess wipes out whole families."

"The Earth cannot punish me for obeying her messenger," Okonkwo said.

"That is true," Obierika agreed. "But if the Oracle said that my son should be killed I would neither dispute it nor be the one to do it."

They would have gone on arguing had Ofoedu not come in just then. It was clear he had important news. Finally, he said:

"The things that happen these days are strange."

"What has happened?" asked Okonkwo.

"Do you know Ogbuefi Ndulue?" Ofoedu asked. "He died this morning."

"That is not strange. He was the oldest man in Ire," said Obierika.

"You are right," Ofoedu agreed. "But you should ask why the drum has not told of his death."

"Why?" asked Obierika and Okonkwo together.

"That is the strange part of it. You know his first wife? When he died this morning, one of his younger wives went to Ozoemena's hut and told her. She rose from her mat, took her stick, and walked to his hut. She knelt on her knees and called her husband three times. Then she went back to her hut. When the youngest wife went to call her to be present at the washing of the body, she was dead."

"That is strange indeed," said Okonkwo. "They will put off Ndulue's funeral until his wife has been buried. That is why the drum has not been beaten."

"It was always said that Ndulue and Ozoemena had one mind," said Obierika. "I remember when I was a young boy, there was a song about them. He could not do anything without telling her."

"I did not know that," said Okonkwo. "I thought he was a strong man in his youth."

"He was indeed," said Ofoedu. Okonkwo shook his head doubtfully.

"He led Umuofia to war in those days," said Obierka.

Okonkwo was beginning to feel like his old self again. All he needed was something to occupy his mind. If he had killed Ikemefuna during the planting season, it would not have been so bad. But now, talking was the next best thing to do. Soon after Ofoedu left, Okonkwo took up his goatskin bag to go.

"I must go home to tap my palm trees for the afternoon," he said.

"It will not be very long now before my in-laws come," said Obierika.

"I shall return very soon," said Okonkwo, looking at the position of the sun.

There were seven men in Obierika's hut when Okonkwo returned. The suitor[14] was a young man of about twenty-five, and with him were his father and his uncle. On Obierika's side were his two elder brothers and Maduka, his sixteen-year-old son.

"Ask Akueke's mother to send us some kola nuts," said Obierika to his son. Maduka vanished into the compound like lightning. The conversation at once centered on him, and everybody agreed he was sharp as a razor.

"I sometimes think he is too sharp," said Obierika, somewhat indulgently. "He hardly ever walks. He is always in a hurry."

"You were much like that yourself," said his eldest brother.

As he was speaking the boy returned, followed by Akueke, his half-sister, carrying a wooden dish with three kola nuts and alligator pepper. She gave the

---

14. suitor a man who is courting a woman

dish and then shook hands, very shyly, with her suitor and his relatives. She was about sixteen and ready for marriage. Her suitor and his relatives surveyed her with expert eyes.

She wore a coiffure[15] done up into a crest in the middle of her head. Cam wood was rubbed lightly into her skin. She wore a black necklace that hung down in three coils. On her arms were red and yellow bangles.

The men had already begun to drink the palm-wine that Akueke's suitor had brought. As the men drank, they talked about everything except why they had gathered. Finally, the suitor's father cleared his voice and announced the purpose of their visit.

Obierika presented him a small bundle of short broomsticks. Ukegbu counted them.

"They are thirty?" he asked.

Obierika nodded in agreement.

"We are at last getting somewhere," Ukegbu said, and then, turning to his brother and his son he said "Let us go out and whisper together." They left, and when they returned, Ukegbu handed the bundle of sticks back. Now there were only fifteen. Obierika passed them to his eldest brother, Machi, who counted them and said:

"We had not thought to go below thirty, but marriage should be a play and not a fight, so we are falling down again." He added ten sticks to the fifteen and gave the bundle to Ukegbu.

In this way, Akueke's bride-price was settled at twenty bags of cowries. It was dusk when the two parties came to this agreement.

"Go and tell Akueke's mother that we have finished," Obierika said to his son, Maduka. Almost immediately, the women came in with a big

---

15. coiffure hairstyle

bowl of *foo-foo*. Obierika's second wife followed with a pot of soup and Maduka brought in a pot of palm-wine.

As the men ate and drank, they talked about the customs of their neighbors.

"It was only this morning," said Obierika, "that Okonkwo and I were talking about Abame and Aninta, where titled men climb trees and pound *foo-foo* for their wives."

"All their customs are upside-down. They do not decide bride-price as we do, with sticks. They haggle and bargain as if they are buying a goat or a cow in the market."

"That is very bad," said Obierika's eldest brother. "But what is good in one place is bad in another place. In Umunso, they do not bargain at all, even with broomsticks. The suitor just goes on bringing bags of cowries until his in-laws tell him to stop. It is a bad custom because it always leads to a quarrel."

"The world is large," said Okonkwo. "I have even heard that in some tribes a man's children belong to his wife and her family."

"It is like the story of white men who, they say, are white like this piece of chalk," said Obierika. He held up a piece of chalk, which every man kept in his hut and with which his guests drew lines on the floor before they ate kola nuts.

"Have you ever seen them?" asked Machi.

"Have you?" asked Obierika.

"One of them passes here frequently," said Machi. "His name is Amadi."

Those who knew Amadi laughed. He was a leper, and the polite name for leprosy was "the white skin."

Chapter 9

For the first time in three nights, Okonkwo slept. He woke up once in the middle of the night and his mind went back to the past three days without making him feel uneasy. He began to wonder why he had felt uneasy. It was like a man wondering in broad daylight why a dream had appeared so terrible to him at night.

Okonkwo turned on his side and went back to sleep. He was roused in the morning by someone banging on his door.

"Who is that?" he growled. He knew it must be Ekwefi. She was the only one who would have the boldness to bang on his door.

"Ezinma is dying," came her voice, and all the tragedy of her life was packed in the words.

Okonkwo sprang from his bed, pushed back the bolt on his door and ran into Ekwefi's hut. Ezinma lay shivering on a mat beside a huge fire that her mother had kept burning all night.

"It is fever," said Okonkwo as he took his machete and went into the bush to collect the leaves and barks that went into the making of medicine for fever.

Ezinma was an only child and the center of her mother's world. Ekwefi even gave her delicacies such as eggs, which children were rarely allowed to eat because such food tempted them to steal. One day as Ezinma was eating an egg, Okonkwo had come in unexpectedly. He was shocked and swore to beat Ekwefi if she dared to give the child eggs again. After Ekwefi was reprimanded, Ezinma developed a keen appetite for eggs. She enjoyed above all the secrecy in which she now ate them. Her mother always took her into their bedroom and shut the door.

Ezinma called her mother by her name, Ekwefi, as grown-up people did. The relationship between them was something like the companionship of equals.

Ekwefi had suffered in her life. She had borne ten children, and nine of them had died in infancy. As she buried one child after another her sorrow gave way to despair and then grim resignation. The birth of her children, which should be a woman's glory, became mere physical agony. Her deepening despair found expression in the names she gave her children: One of them was Onwumbiko—"Death, I implore you." But Death took no notice; Onwumbiko died in his fifteenth month. Ekwefi became defiant and called her next child Onwuma—"Death may please himself." And he did.

After the death of Ekwefi's second child, Okonkwo went to a medicine man, who told him the child was an *ogbanje*[16] one of those wicked children who, when they died, entered their mother to be born again.

"When your wife becomes pregnant again," the medicine man said, "let her not sleep in her hut. Let her go and stay with her people. In that way, she will break the evil cycle of birth and death."

Ekwefi did this. As soon as she became pregnant, she went to live with her mother. The child was Onwumbiko. He was not given a proper burial when he died. Okonkwo called in another medicine man famous for his great knowledge of *ogbanje* children. He asked Okonkwo a few questions.

"On what day was it born?"

"*Oye,*"[17] replied Okonkwo.

"And it died this morning?" Okonkwo said yes, and only then realized the child had died on the same day as it had been born. The neighbors also saw the coincidence. The medicine man ordered

---

16. *ogbanje* a child who repeatedly dies and returns to his or her mother to be reborn

17. *Oye* the name of one of the four market days

there would be no mourning for the dead child. He took a sharp razor and cut it. Then he took it away to bury in the Evil Forest, dragging it behind him. After such treatment, it would think twice before coming again, unless it was one of the stubborn ones.

By the time Onwumbiko died, Ekwefi was a bitter woman. Her husband's first wife had already had three sons, all strong and healthy. Ekwefi had nothing but good wishes for her. But she had grown so bitter about her own *chi* that she could not rejoice with others over their good fortune. When Nwoye's mother celebrated the birth of her sons, Ekwefi was the only unhappy one. The other wife took this for ill-will. How could she know that Ekwefi's bitterness did not flow to others but to her own soul; that she did not blame others for their good fortune but her own evil *chi* who denied her any?

At last Ezinma was born, and although she was ailing, she seemed determined to live. At first, Ekwefi accepted her with resignation. But when she lived to her sixth year, love returned once more to the mother, as well as anxiety. She determined to nurse this child to health. She was rewarded by occasional spells of health. But all of a sudden, Ezinma would go down again. Everyone knew she was an *ogbanje*. But she had lived so long perhaps she had decided to stay. Some *ogbanje* did take pity on their mothers, and stayed. Ekwefi believed deep inside that Ezinma had come to stay. Her faith had been strengthened a year before when a medicine man had dug up Ezinma's *iyi-uwa*.[18]

Ezinma's *iyi-uwa* was a smooth pebble wrapped in a dirty rag. The man who dug it up was Okagbue, who was famous for his knowledge in these matters.

---

18. ***iyi-uwa*** a special kind of stone that links the *ogbanje* and the spirit world; if the *iyi-uwa* is discovered and destroyed, the child will live.

"Where did you bury your *iyi-uwa*?" he had asked Ezinma. She was nine then and recovering from a serious illness.

"What is that?" she asked.

"You know what it is. You buried it in the ground so that you can die and return to torment your mother."

Ezinma looked at her mother, whose sad, pleading eyes were fixed on her.

The medicine man turned again to Ezinma. "Where did you bury your *iyi-uwa?*"

"Where they bury children," she said. They set out with Ezinma leading the way. At the main road, Ezinma turned left. The crowd followed her silently. Ezinma turned left into the bush and the crowd followed her. Then she suddenly turned round and began to walk back to the road, and then back home.

"Where did you bury your *iyi-uwa?*" asked Okagbue when Ezinma stopped by her father's hut.

"It is near that orange tree," she said.

"And why did you not say so, you wicked daughter?" Okonkwo swore furiously. The medicine man ignored him.

"Come and show me the exact spot," he said quietly to Ezinma.

"It is here," she said when they got to the tree. She touched the ground with her finger.

"Bring me a hoe," said Okagbue. Ekwefi brought it, and he set to work digging a pit. The pit grew deeper and deeper. Okagbue worked tirelessly and in silence. Neighbors stood around, watching. The pit was now so deep they no longer saw the digger. Suddenly, Okagbue sprang to the surface. "It is very near now," he said. "I have felt it. Call your wife and child," he said to Okonkwo. Then he went back to the pit. After a few more hoe-fuls of earth, he struck the *iyi-uwa*. He raised it carefully with the hoe and threw it to the surface. Some ran away in fear when it was thrown. But they soon returned and everyone was gazing at the rag. Okagbue emerged. He untied the rag and the smooth, shiny pebble fell out.

"Is this yours?" he asked Ezinma.

"Yes," she replied. All the women shouted with joy because Ekwefi's troubles were at last ended.

This had happened more than a year before and Ezinma had not been ill since. And then suddenly she had begun to shiver in the night. Ekwefi built a fire. But Ezinma got worse and worse. Ekwefi knelt by her, praying a thousand times. Her husband's wives said it was only fever. She did not hear them.

Okonkwo returned from the bush carrying a large bundle of grasses and leaves, medicinal roots and barks. He went into Ekwefi's hut and sat down. "Get me a pot," he said, "and leave the child alone."

Ekwefi brought the pot and Okonkwo selected the best from the bundle and put them in the pot. Ekwefi poured in water.

"Is that enough?" she asked when she poured in about half the water in the bowl.

"A little more. . . I said a *little*. Are you deaf?" Okonkwo roared at her. Then he stood to return to his hut. "You must watch the pot carefully, and don't allow it to boil over. If it does, its power will be gone." Ekwefi began to tend the medicine pot. Her eyes went constantly from Ezinma to the boiling pot and back to Ezinma.

Okonkwo returned when he felt the medicine had cooked long enough. He took down the pot and roused Ezinma and placed her astride the steaming pot.

Ezinma struggled to escape but was held down. Ekwefi mopped her as she lay down and was soon asleep.

Chapter 10

Large crowds began to gather on the village green when the edge had worn off the sun's heat. Most ceremonies took place at that time of day. It was clear from the way the crowd stood that the ceremony was for men. The women looked on like outsiders. The titled men and elders sat on their stools waiting for the trials to begin. In front of the men was a row of nine empty stools. Two groups of people stood at a distance beyond the stools. They faced the elders. There were three men in one group and three men and one woman in the other. The woman was Mgbafo and the three men with her were her brothers. In the other group were her husband, Uzowulu, and his relatives.

An iron gong sounded. Then came the throaty and awesome voices of the *egwugwu.*[19] The drum sounded again and the flute blew. The air was filled with trembling voices as the spirits of the ancestors greeted themselves in their strange language. The special house from which they emerged faced the forest, away from the crowd. The crowd saw only its back with the many-colored patterns and drawings done by specially chosen women. These women never saw the inside of the hut. No woman ever did. No woman ever asked questions about the most secret cult in the clan.

---

19. ***egwugwu*** a man who impersonates one of the ancestral spirits of the village

The voices flew around the dark, closed hut like tongues of fire. The ancestral spirits of the clan were abroad. Then the *egwugwu* appeared. The women and children ran. It was instinctive. When nine of the greatest masked spirits in the clan came out together, it was terrifying.

Each of the nine *egwugwu* represented a village of the clan. The nine villages of Umuofia had grown out of the nine sons of the first father of the clan. Evil Forest, the leader, represented the village of Umueru, or the children of Eru, who was the eldest of the nine sons.

"*Umuofia kwenu!*" shouted the leading *egwugwu,* pushing the air with his arms. The elders of the clan replied, "*Yaa!*"

Evil Forest then thrust the pointed end of his staff into the earth. It began to shake and rattle. He took the first of the empty stools and the eight other *egwugwu* began to sit in order of seniority after him.

Okonkwo's wives might have noticed that the second *egwugwu* had the springy walk of Okonkwo. They might also have noticed that Okonkwo was not sitting among the elders and titled men. But if they thought these things, they kept them to themselves.

The *egwugwu* with the springy walk looked terrible, with a huge wooden face painted white except for the round hollow eyes and the charred teeth as big as a man's fingers. On his head were two powerful horns.

Evil Forest addressed the two groups of people facing them. "Uzowulu's body, I salute you," he said. Spirits always addressed humans as "bodies." Uzowulu bent down and touched the earth with his hand as a sign of submission.

Evil Forest turned to the other group and addressed the eldest of the three brothers. The hearing then began.

Uzowulu presented his case. "That woman Mgbafo is my wife. I married her with my money and my yams. I do not owe my in-laws anything. One day they came to my house, beat me and took my wife and children away. I have waited for my wife to return. At last, I went to my in-laws and said to them, "You have taken back your sister. I did not send her away. The law of the clan is that you should return her bride-price. But my wife's brother said they had nothing to tell me. So I have brought the matter to the fathers of the clan. I salute you."

"Your words are good," said the leader of the *egwugwu*. "Let us hear Odukwe. His words may also be good."

"What my in-law has told you is true. However, my in-law, Uzowulu, is a beast. My sister lived with him for nine years. During those years, no day passed without him beating the woman. Two years ago, when she was pregnant, he beat her until she miscarried."

"It is a lie!" Uzowulu shouted.

"Last year when my sister was recovering from an illness, he beat her again. If the neighbors had not gone in, she would have been killed. In this case, she ran to save her life. Her two children belong to Uzowulu. We do not dispute it, but they are too young to leave their mother. If Uzowulu should agree to change and beg her to return, she will do so on the understanding that he never beat her again."

Evil Forest called witnesses, who both agreed about the beating. Then the nine *egwugwu* went to consult in their house. The metal gong sounded. The *egwugwu* reappeared. Evil Forest began to speak.

"We have heard both sides of the case," said Evil Forest. "Our duty is not to blame this man or to praise him, but to settle the dispute." He turned to Uzowulu's group and said to Uzowulu:

"Go to your in-laws with a pot of wine and beg your wife to return. It is not bravery when a man fights with a woman." He turned to Odukwe to greet him.

While they spoke, two other groups of people had replaced the first, and a great land case began.

Chapter 11

The night was black as charcoal. Ezinma and her mother sat on a mat after their supper of yam *foo-foo* and bitter-leaf soup. A palm-oil lamp gave out yellowish light. Without it, it would have been impossible to eat; one could not have known where one's mouth was in the darkness of that night. There was an oil lamp in all four huts on Okonkwo's compound, and each hut seen from the others looked like a soft eye of yellow half-light.

The world was silent except for the shrill cry of insects and the sound of Nwayieke's mortar and pestle[20] as she pounded her *foo-foo*. Nwayieke's late cooking was also part of the night.

Okonkwo had eaten from his wives' dishes and was now reclining with his back against the wall. Low voices, broken now and again by singing, reached Okonkwo from his wives' huts as each woman and her children told folk stories. Ekwefi and her daughter, Ezinma, sat on a mat on the floor.

Ezinma was beginning a story when a loud and

---

20. pestle a club-shaped tool for grinding or mashing substances in a mortar, or bowl high-pitched voice broke the silence of the night. It was Chielo, the priestess of Agbala, who was prophesying. Tonight, she was addressing her prophesy to Okonkwo, and so everyone in his family listened. The folk stories stopped.

The voice came like a sharp knife cutting through the night. Ekwefi heard Ezinma's name and jerked her head sharply like an animal that had sniffed death in the air. Her heart jumped painfully.

The priestess had reached Okonkwo's compound and was saying again and again that Agbala wanted to see his daughter, Ezinma. Okonkwo pleaded with the priestess to come back in the morning. Chielo ignored him and went on shouting that Agbala wanted to see his daughter. Okonkwo was still pleading. The priestess screamed. "Beware, Okonkwo!" she warned. "Does a man speak when a god speaks? Beware!"

The priestess walked straight toward Ekwefi's hut. Okonkwo came after her.

"Ekwefi," she called, "Agbala greets you. Where is my daughter, Ezinma? Agbala wants to see her."

Ekwefi came out carrying her oil lamp. "Where does Agbala want to see her?" Ekwefi asked.

"Where else but in his house in the hills and the caves?" replied the priestess.

"I will come with you, too," Ekwefi said firmly.

The priestess cursed, her voice cracking like thunder. "How dare you, woman, to go before the mighty Agbala of your own accord? Beware, lest he strike you in his anger. Bring me my daughter."

Ekwefi went into the hut and came out with Ezinma.

"Come, my daughter," said the priestess. "I shall carry you on my back."

Ezinma began to cry. She was used to Chielo calling her "my daughter," but this was a different Chielo she now saw in the yellow half-light.

"Don't be afraid," said Ekwefi stroking her head. They went outside again. The priestess bent down on one knee and Ezinma climbed on her back.

Chielo began once again to chant greetings to her god. She turned and walked through Okonkwo's hut. Ezinma was crying loudly now, calling on her mother. The two voices disappeared in the darkness.

"Why do you stand there as though Ezinma had been kidnapped?" asked Okonkwo.

But Ekwefi did not hear. She stood for a while, and then made up her mind. She hurried outside. "Where are you going?" Okonkwo asked.

"I am following Chielo," she replied and disappeared in the darkness.

The priestess's voice was already growing faint. Ekwefi hurried in the direction of the voice. She picked her way easily on the footpath. She began to run, and she hit her foot against an outcropped root. Terror seized her. It was an ill omen. She ran faster. Chielo's voice was still a long way away. Ekwefi tripped, then she realized that Chielo's chanting had stopped. Her heart beat violently. Then Chielo's voice came from a few paces ahead, but Ekwefi could not see Chielo. But she heard the chanting and trudged behind, neither getting too near nor keeping too far back. Now that she walked slowly, she had time to think. What would she do when they got to the cave? She would not dare to enter. She would be all alone in that fearful place. She thought of all the terrors of the night, those evil qualities set free upon the world.

The priestess's voice came at longer intervals now. The air was cool and damp. Ezinma sneezed. Ekwefi muttered, "Life to you." At the same time, the priestess said "Life to you, my daughter."

The priestess screamed. "Somebody is walking behind me!" she said. "Whether you are spirit or man, may Agbala twist your neck until you see your heels!"

Ekwefi stood rooted to the spot. She stood until Chielo had increased the distance between them, then Ekwefi began to follow again. It occurred to her that they could not have been heading for the cave. They must be going toward Umuachi, the farthest village in the clan.

Ekwefi heard the cries of Chielo. The priestess was now saluting the village of Umuachi. It was unbelievable, the distance they had covered. As they emerged into the open village, it became possible to see the vague shape of trees.

Chielo's voice was now rising continuously. Ekwefi had a feeling of openness, and she guessed they must be in the village green. Chielo passed by as Ekwefi quickly moved from her line of retreat, and they began to go back the way they had come.

It was a long and weary journey. Ekwefi could now see the figure of the priestess and her burden, and she slowed down. Ekwefi had prayed for the moon to rise, but the half-light was more terrifying than darkness. The world was now peopled with vague, fantastic figures. At one stage, Ekwefi was so afraid she nearly called out to Chielo for human sympathy. Then Chielo's voice rose again in her possessed chanting. Ekwefi recoiled because there was no humanity there. It was not the same Chielo who sat with her in market. It was the priestess of Agbala, the Oracle of the Hills and Caves.

At last, they turned and began to head for the caves. From then on, Chielo never ceased in her chanting. She greeted her god in many names—the owner of the future, the god who cut a man down when life was sweetest to him.

The moon was now up, and she could see Chielo and Ezinma clearly. How a woman could carry a child of that size so easily and for so long was a miracle. But Ekwefi was not thinking about that. Chielo was not a woman that night.

As soon as the priestess stepped into the ring of hills, her voice was doubled in strength and thrown back on all sides. It was indeed the shrine of a great god. Ekwefi was beginning to doubt the wisdom of her coming. Nothing would happen to Ezinma, she thought. And if anything did, could she stop it? Ekwefi would not dare to enter the underground cave. Her coming was quite useless, she thought.

As these things went through her mind, she did not realize how close they were to the cave mouth. When the priestess, with Ezinma on her back, disappeared through a hole hardly big enough to pass a hen, Ekwefi broke into a run as though to stop them. As she stood gazing at the darkness that had swallowed them, tears gushed from her eyes. Ekwefi swore that if she heard Ezinma cry she would rush into the cave to defend her against all the gods in the world. She would die with her.

Having sworn that oath, Ekwefi sat down and waited. Her fear had vanished. She could hear the priestess's voice. She buried her face in her lap and waited.

Ekwefi did not know how long she waited. It must have been a very long time. She heard a noise behind her and turned sharply. A man stood there with a machete in his hand. Ekwefi screamed and sprang to her feet.

"Don't be foolish," said Okonkwo's voice. "I thought you were going into the shrine with Chielo," he mocked.

Ekwefi did not answer. Tears of gratitude filled her eyes. She knew her daughter was safe.

"Go home and sleep," said Okonkwo. "I shall wait."

"I shall wait too. It is almost dawn."

As they stood there together, Ekwefi's mind went back to the days when they were young. She had married Anene because Okonkwo was too poor then to marry. Two years after her marriage to Anene, she could bear it no longer and ran away to Okonkwo. It had been early in the morning. The moon was shining. She was going to the stream to fetch water. Okonkwo's house was on the way to the stream. She went in and knocked at his door and he came out. Even in those days, he was not a man of many words. He just carried her inside.

Chapter 12

The next morning, the neighborhood wore a festive air because Okonkwo's friend, Obierika, was celebrating his daughter's *uri.*[21] Her bride-price had been paid. Her suitor now would bring palm-wine to her parents but also to a large group of kinsmen. Everybody had been invited. But it was really a woman's ceremony, and the central figures were the bride and her mother.

Breakfast was eaten hastily, and women and children gathered at Obierka's compound to help the

---

21. ***uri*** part of the engagement ceremony when the dowry, or bride-price, is paid

bride's mother in her difficult but happy task of cooking for the village.

Okonkwo's family was astir[22] like any other. Nwoye's mother carried a basket of coco-yams, a cake of salt, and fish to present to Obierka's wife. Okonkwo's youngest wife had a basket of plantains and coco-yams and a small pot of palm-oil.

Ekwefi was exhausted from the previous night. It was not very long since they all had returned. The priestess, with Ezinma sleeping on her back, had crawled out of the shrine on her belly. She looked straight ahead of her and walked back to the village. Okonkwo and Ekwefi followed at a respectful distance. She went to Ekwefi's hut, placed Ezinma carefully on her bed, and left without a word.

Ekwefi asked Nwoye's mother to explain that she would be late. Her food was not ready, and she must wait for Ezinma to wake.

As they spoke, Ezinma emerged, rubbing her eyes and stretching. She saw the other children with their water-pots and went back for her pot.

"Have you slept enough?" asked her mother.

"Yes," she replied. "Let us go."

"Not before you have had your breakfast," said Ekwefi. And she went into her hut to warm soup.

"I will tell Obierka's wife you are coming later," Nwoye's mother said, then they left.

As they trooped through Okonkwo's hut, he asked: "Who shall prepare my afternoon meal?"

"I shall return to do it," said Ojiugo.

Okonkwo was also feeling tired, for he had not slept at all the previous night. He had felt very anxious but did not show it. When Ekwefi had followed the priestess, he had waited for a manly interval to pass and then had gone to the shrine,

---

22. astir in motion

where he thought they must be. It occurred to him that the priestess might have chosen to go around the villages first. Okonkwo had returned home and sat waiting. When he thought he had waited long enough, he returned to the shrine. It was only on his fourth trip that he had found Ekwefi. By then, he was gravely worried.

Obierka's compound was as busy as an anthill. Temporary cooking tripods were on every space, and *foo-foo* was pounded in a hundred wooden mortars. Some women cooked yams and cassava; others prepared vegetable soup.

Three young men helped Obierika slaughter two goats with which the soup was made. The fattest goat, as big as a small cow, was the one Obierika would present live to his in-laws.

One of Obierka's relatives had gone to the market of Umuike to buy the goat. "It is a wonderful place," the relative said.

"It is the result of a great medicine," said Obierika. "The people of Umuike made a powerful medicine. Every market day, this medicine stands on the market ground in the shape of an old woman with a fan. With this magic fan she beckons to the market all the neighboring clans."

Early in the afternoon, the first two pots of palm-wine arrived from Obierika's in-laws. When the heat of the sun began to soften, Obierika's son, Maduka, swept the ground in front of his father's hut. As if they had been waiting for that, Obierika's relatives and friends began to arrive. Some came carrying carved wooden stools. Okonkwo was one of them.

"I hope our in-laws will bring many pots of wine," said Ezenwa. "They come from a village known to be selfish, but they ought to know Akeuke is the bride for a king."

"They dare not bring fewer than thirty pots," Okonkwo said. "I shall tell them my mind if they do."

At that moment, Obierika's son, Maduka, led out the giant goat. They all admired it and said it was the way things should be done.

Very soon after, the in-laws began to arrive. Young men and boys in single file, each carrying a pot of wine, came first. Obierika's relatives counted them. Twenty, twenty-five. There was a long break, and the hosts looked at each other as if to say, "I told you." Then more pots came. Thirty, thirty-five. The hosts nodded in approval and seemed to say, "Now they are behaving like men." Altogether, there were fifty pots of wine. Next came Ibe, the suitor, and elders of his family. Then the bride, her mother, and half a dozen women and girls emerged. The married women wore their best clothes and the girls wore red and black waist-beads and anklets of brass.

The kola was eaten and the drinking of palm-wine began. Groups of four or five men sat round with a pot in their midst. As the evening wore on, food was presented to the guests. There were huge bowls of *foo-foo* and steaming pots of soup. There were also pots of yam stew. It was a great feast.

As night fell, burning torches were set on wooden tripods and the young men raised a song. The elders sat in a big circle and the singers went round singing each man's praise. They had something to say for every man. Some were great farmers, some were speakers for the clan. Okonkwo was the greatest wrestler and warrior alive. The girls came from the inner compound to dance. At first, the bride was not among them. When she finally appeared, holding a chicken in her right hand, a loud cheer rose from the crowd. All the other dancers made way for her. She presented the chicken to the musicians and began to dance. Her brass anklets rattled as she danced, and her body gleamed with cam wood in the soft yellow light. The musicians with their wood, clay, and metal instruments went from song to song.

It was very late when the guests rose to go, taking their bride home to spend seven weeks with her suitor's family. They sang songs as they went. On their way, they paid courtesy visits to important men like Okonkwo, before they finally left for their village. Okonkwo gave them a present of two chickens.

Chapter 13

Go-di-di-go-go-di-go. It was the *ekwe*[23] talking. One of the things every man learned was the language of the hollowed-out wooden instrument. The cannon boomed at intervals.

Umuofia was still swallowed up in sleep and silence when the *ekwe* began to talk, and the cannon shattered the silence. Men stirred on their bamboo beds and listened anxiously. Somebody was dead. The faint and distant wailing of women settled like sorrow on the earth. Now and again, a deeper cry

23. *ekwe* musical instrument; a type of drum made of wood

rose above the wailing when a man came into the place of death. He raised his voice once or twice in manly sorrow and then sat with the other men listening to the endless wailing of the women and the language of the *ekwe*. Now and then the cannons boomed. The *ekwe* carried the news to all the nine villages and beyond. It began by naming the clan: *Umuofia obodo dike*, "the land of the brave." It said this over and over again. Anxiety mounted in every heart that hovered on a bamboo bed that night. It went nearer and named the village: *"Iguedo of the yellow grinding-stone!"* It was Okonkwo's village. At last, the man was named and people sighed "E-u-u, Ezeudu is dead." A cold shiver ran down Okonkwo's back as he remembered the last time the old man had visited him. "That boy calls you father," he had said of Ikemefuna. "Bear no hand in his death."

Ezeudu was a great man, and so all the clan was at his funeral. The ancient drums of death were beaten, guns and cannon were fired, and men dashed about in frenzy. It was a warrior's funeral, and from morning until night warriors came and went in their age groups. They all wore palm-fiber skirts and their bodies were painted with chalk and charcoal. Now and again an ancestral spirit or *egwugwu* appeared. Some of them were very violent. There had been a mad rush when one had appeared with a machete and was only prevented from doing serious harm by two men who restrained him. He sang, in a terrifying voice, that Ekwensu, or Evil Spirit, had entered his eye.

But some of the *egwugwu* were quite harmless. One was so old and weak he leaned heavily on a stick.

He walked unsteadily to the place where the corpse was laid, gazed at it, and went away again—to the underworld.

The land of the living was not far from the domain of the ancestors. There was coming and going between them, especially at festivals and also when an old man died, because an old man was very close to the ancestors.

Ezeudu had been the oldest man in the village, and at his death, there were only three men in the entire clan who were older, and four or five others his age. Whenever one of these ancient men appeared in the crowd to dance the funeral steps of the tribe, younger men gave way.

It was a great funeral, as befitted a noble warrior. Ezeudu had taken three titles in his life. It was a rare achievement. There were only four titles in the clan, and only one or two men in any generation achieved the fourth and highest. Because he had taken titles, Ezeudu was to be buried after dark.

Before this quiet and final rite, the frenzy increased tenfold. Drums beat violently, and men leaped up and down. It was then that the one-handed spirit came, carrying a basket of water. People made way for him on all sides and the noise subsided.

"Ezeudu!" he said in his deep voice. "If you had been poor, I would have asked you to be rich when you come again. But you were rich. If you had been a coward, I would have asked you to bring courage. But you were fearless. If you had died young, I would have asked you to get life. But you lived long. So I shall ask you to come again the way you came before." He danced a few more steps and went away.

The drums and dancing began again and reached fever-heat. Darkness was around the corner, and the burial was near. Guns fired the last salute. From the center of the fury came a cry of agony and shouts of horror. All was silent. In the center of the crowd, a boy lay in a pool of blood. It was the dead man's sixteen-year-old son, who with his brothers and half-brothers had been dancing the traditional farewell to their father. Okonkwo's gun had exploded. A piece of iron had pierced the boy's heart.

The confusion that followed was without parallel in the tradition of Umuofia. Violent deaths were frequent, but nothing like this had ever happened.

The only course open to Okonkwo was to flee from the clan. It was a crime against the earth goddess to kill a clansman, and a man who committed such a crime must flee from the land. Crime was of two kinds, male and female. Okonkwo had committed the female crime, because he had not meant to kill. He could return to the clan after seven years.

That night he collected his most valuable belongings into head-loads. His wives wept bitterly and their children wept without knowing why. Obierika and half a dozen friends came to help. They each made nine or ten trips carrying Okonkwo's yams to store in Obierika's barn. Before the cock crowed, Okonkwo and his family were fleeing to his motherland. It was a little village called Mbanta, just beyond the borders of Mbaino.

As soon as the day broke, a large crowd of men from Ezeudu's quarter stormed Okonkwo's compound, dressed for war. They set fire to his houses, killed his animals, and destroyed his barn. It was the justice of the earth goddess, and they were merely her messengers. They had no hatred against Okonkwo.

His greatest friend, Okierika, was among them. They were merely cleansing the land Okonkwo had polluted with the blood of a clansman.

Obierika was a man who thought about things. When the will of the goddess had been done, he sat down in his hut and mourned his friend's calamity.[24] Why should a man suffer for an offense he had not meant to commit? Although he thought a long time, he found no answer. He was merely led into greater complexities. He remembered his wife's twins, whom he had thrown away. What crime had they committed? The Earth had decreed that they were an offense and must be destroyed. If the clan did not enforce punishment, her wrath was loosed on all the land and not just on the offender.

---

24. *calamity* tragedy or severe loss

Part 2 In the Village of Mbanta

Chapter 14

Okonkwo was well received by his mother's kinsmen in Mbanta. The old man who received him was his mother's younger brother, now the eldest member of that family. His name was Uchendu, and it was he who had received Okonkwo's mother thirty years before when she had been brought home from Umuofia to be buried with her people. Okonkwo was only a boy then and Uchendu still remembered him crying the traditional farewell: "Mother, mother, mother is going."

Today, Okonkwo was taking his family of three wives and their children to seek refuge in his motherland. As soon as Uchendu saw him with his sad and weary company, he guessed what had happened, and asked no questions. It was not until the following day that Okonkwo told him the full story. The old men listened silently to the end and said with some relief, "It is a female crime."

Okonkwo was given a plot of ground on which to build his compound, and two or three pieces of land on which to farm during the coming planting season. With the help of his mother's kinsmen, he built a hut for himself and three huts for his wives. Each of Uchendu's five sons gave three hundred seed-yams to enable their cousin to plant a farm.

At last, the rain came. It was sudden and tremendous. All the grass had long been scorched brown, and the sands felt like live coals to the feet. Then came the clap of thunder. It was an angry and thirsty clap, unlike the liquid rumbling of the rainy season. A mighty wind arose and filled the air with dust. Palm trees swayed as the wind combed their leaves into flying crests.

When the rain finally came, it was in large solid drops of frozen water the people called "the nuts of the water of heaven." They were hard and painful on the body as they fell, yet young people ran about happily picking up the cold nuts and throwing them into their mouths to melt.

The earth quickly came to life and the birds in the forest chirped merrily. A vague scent of life and green vegetation was in the air. As the rain began to fall more quietly, in smaller liquid drops, children sought shelter, and all were happy, refreshed, and thankful.

Okonkwo and his family worked very hard to plant a new farm. But it was like beginning life anew. Work no longer had the pleasure it used to have, and when there was no work to do he sat in a silent half-sleep.

His life had been ruled by a great passion—to become one of the lords of the clan. He had all but achieved it. Then everything had been broken. He had been cast out of his clan like a fish onto a dry, sandy beach. Clearly, his *chi* was not meant for great things. A man could not rise beyond the destiny of his *chi*. The saying of the elders was not true—that if a man said yes, his *chi* said yes. Here was a man whose *chi* said no despite his saying yes.

The old man, Uchendu, saw clearly that Okonkwo had yielded to despair, and he was greatly troubled. He would speak to him after the upcoming marriage ceremony.

The youngest of Uchendu's five sons, Amikwu, was marrying a new wife. The bride-price had been paid. All but the last ceremony had been performed. Amikwu and his people had taken palm-wine to the bride's kinsmen about two moons before Okonkwo's arrival in Mbanta. So it was time for the final ceremony.

The daughters of the family were all there, some of them having come a long way from their homes in distant villages. Uchendu's eldest daughter had come from Obodo, nearly half a day away. It was a full gathering of the family, in the same way as they would meet if a death had occurred in the family. There were twenty-two of them.

They sat in a big circle on the ground and the bride sat in the center with a hen in her right hand. Uchendu sat by her, holding the ancestral staff of the family. Others stood outside the circle, watching.

Uchendu's eldest daughter, Njide, asked the questions.

"Remember, if you do not answer truthfully, you will suffer or even die at childbirth," she began. "How many men have been with you since my brother first said he wanted to marry you?"

"None," she answered simply.

"Swear on this staff of my fathers," said Uchendu.

She did. Uchendu took the hen from her, slit its throat with a sharp knife and allowed some of the blood to fall on his ancestral staff.

From that day, Amikwu took the young bride to his hut, and she became his wife.

On the second day, Uchendu called together his sons and daughters and his nephew, Okonkwo. Uchendu pulled gently at his gray beard and gnashed his teeth. He began to speak quietly, picking his words with great care:

"It is Okonkwo that I primarily wish to speak to," he began. "But I want all of you to note what I am going to say. Why is Okonkwo with us today? This is not his clan. He does not belong here. He is an exile, condemned for seven years to live in a strange land. So he is bowed with grief. But there is just one question I would like to ask him. Can you tell me, Okonkwo, why one of the commonest names we give our children is Nneka, or 'Mother is Supreme?' We all know a man is the head of the family and his wives do his bidding. A child belongs to its father and his family and not to its mother and her family. Yet, we say Nneka—'Mother is Supreme.' Why is that?"

There was silence. "I want Okonkwo to answer me," said Uchendu.

"I do not know the answer," Okonkwo replied.

"You do not know the answer? So you see you are a child. You have many wives and children—more children than I have. You are a great man in your clan. But you are still a child, my child. Listen to me and I shall tell you. But there is one more question I shall ask you. Why is it that when a woman dies, she is taken home to be buried with her own kinsmen?"

Okonkwo shook his head.

"He does not know that either," said Uchendu, "and yet he is full of sorrow because he has come to live in his motherland for a few years." He turned to his sons and daughters. "Can you answer my question?"

They all shook their heads.

"Listen to me," he said. "It's true that a child belongs to its father. But when a father beats his child, it seeks sympathy in its mother's hut. A man belongs to his fatherland when things are good and life is sweet. But when there is sorrow, he finds refuge in his motherland. That is why we say that the mother is supreme. Your mother is there to protect you. Is it right that you, Okonkwo, should bring to your mother a heavy heart and refuse to be comforted? Be careful or you may displease the dead." He paused for a long while. "These are now your kinsmen." He waved at his sons and daughters. "You think you are the greatest sufferer in the world? Do you know men are sometimes banished for life? I had six wives once. I have none now except that young girl. Do you know how many children I have buried? Twenty-two. I did not hang myself. If you think you are the greatest sufferer in the world, ask my daughter, Akueni, how many twins she has borne and thrown away. I have no more to say to you."

Chapter 15

In the second year of Okonkwo's exile, his friend Obierika came to visit him. He brought two young men, each carrying a heavy bag on his head. Okonkwo helped them put down their loads. The bags were full of cowries.

Okonkwo was very happy to receive his friend. So were his wives and children, and his cousins and their wives.

Uchendu had been told that three strangers had come to Okonkwo's house. He held out his hands to them when they came into his hut.

"This is Obierika, my great friend," Okonkwo said to Uchendu. "I have already spoken to you about him."

"Yes," said the old man, turning to Obierika. "My son has told me about you, and I am happy you have come to see us. I knew your father, Iweka. He was a great man. He had many friends here and came to see them quite often. Those were good days when men had friends in distant clans. Your generation does not know that. You stay at home, afraid of your next-door neighbor." He got up and came back with a kola nut.

"Go into that room," he said to Okonkwo, pointing with his finger. "You will find a pot of wine there."

Okonkwo brought the wine and they began to drink. It was a day old and very strong.

"Yes," said Uchendu after a long silence. "People traveled more in those days. I know all the clans—Aninta, Umuazu, Ikeocha, Elumelu, Abame—I know them all."

"Have you heard," asked Okierika, "that Abame is no more?"

"How is that?" asked Uchendu and Okonkwo together.

"Abame has been wiped out," said Obierika. "It is a strange and terrible story. If I had not seen the few survivors with my own eyes and heard their story with my own ears, I would not have believed."

"Three moons ago," said Obierika, "a little band of fugitives came into our town. Most were sons of mothers who had been buried with us. But there were others who had nowhere else to go." He drank his palm-wine, and Okonkwo filled his horn again.

"During the last planting season, a white man had appeared in their clan."

"An albino," suggested Okonkwo.

"He was not an albino. He was quite different. He was riding an iron horse. Many ran away, but the fearless ones went near and even touched him. The elders consulted their Oracle and it told them that the strange man would break their clan and spread destruction among them. As a result, they killed the white man and tied his iron horse to their sacred tree because it looked as if it would run away to call the man's friends. I forgot to tell you another thing the Oracle said. It said that other white men were on their way. The first man was sent to explore our land, so they killed him."

"What did the white man say before they killed him?" asked Uchendu?

"He said something, only they did not understand him," said Obierika. "He spoke through his nose. Anyway, they killed him. That was before planting season. For a long time nothing happened. Then one morning three white men led by a band of ordinary men like us came to the clan. They saw the iron horse and went away again. Most of the people of Abame had gone to their farms. Only a few saw these white men. For many weeks, nothing else happened. They have a big market in Abame every other week, and the whole clan gathers. That was the day it happened. The three white men and a very large number of other men surrounded the market. They must have used powerful medicine to make themselves invisible. Then they began to shoot. Everybody was killed except the old and the sick who were at home and a handful of men and women whose *chi* was wide awake and brought them out of that market." He paused.

"Their clan is now completely empty. Even the sacred fish in their mysterious lake have fled, and the water is the color of blood. A great evil has come upon their land as the Oracle had warned."

There was a long silence. Uchendu ground his teeth together. Then he burst out, "Never kill a man who says nothing. Those men of Abame were fools. What did they know about the man?"

"They were fools," said Okonkwo after a pause.

"They had been warned that danger was ahead. They should have armed themselves with their guns and their machetes even when they went to market."

"They have paid for their foolishness," said Obierika. "But I am greatly afraid. We have heard stories about white men who made powerful guns and took slaves away across the sea, but no one thought the stories were true."

"There is no story that is not true," said Uchendu. "The world has no end, and what is good among one people is an evil with others."

Okonkwo's first wife soon set before their guests a big meal of pounded yams and bitter-leaf soup. Nwoye brought in a pot of sweet wine. Ezinma brought a bowl of water with which to wash their hands. Then they began to eat and drink the wine. When they had eaten, Obierika pointed at the two heavy bags.

"That is the money from your yams," he said. "I sold the big ones as soon as you left. Later I sold some of the seed-yams and gave out others to sharecroppers. I shall do that every year until you return. But I thought you would need the money now and so I brought it. Who knows what may happen tomorrow? Perhaps green men will come to our clan and shoot us."

"I do not know how to thank you," said Okonkwo.

"I can tell you," said Obierika "Kill one of your sons for me."

"That will not be enough," said Okonkwo.

"Then kill yourself," said Obierika.

"Forgive me," said Okonkwo, smiling. "I shall not talk about thanking you anymore."

Chapter 16

Two years later, Obierika paid another visit to his friend in exile. The circumstances were less happy. The missionaries had come to Umuofia. They had built their church there, had won a handful of converts, and were already sending missionaries to the surrounding villages. That was a source of great sorrow to the leaders of the clan, but many believed the strange faith would not last. None of the converts was a man whose word was heeded.[25] None was a man of title. They were mostly empty men the clan called *efulefu*.[26] In the language of the clan, an *efulefu* was a man who sold his machete and wore the sheath to battle.

What moved Obierika to visit Okonkwo was the sudden appearance of Nwoye, Okonkwo's son, among the missionaries in Umuofia.

"What are you doing here?" Obierika had asked when he was finally allowed to talk to Nwoye.

"I am one of them," replied Nwoye.

"How is your father?" Obierika asked, not knowing what else to say.

"I don't know. He is not my father," said Nwoye, unhappily. When he heard this, Obierika went to Mbanta to see his friend. There, he found that Okonkwo did not want to speak about Nwoye. It was only from Nwoye's mother that he heard scraps of the story.

The missionaries had caused a stir in the village of Mbanta. There were six, and one was a white man. Everyone came to see the white man. Stories about

---

25. heeded followed or listened to
26. *efulefu* worthless man

these strange men had grown since one had been killed in Abame. Everybody was at home. The harvest was over.

When they had gathered, the white interpreter began to speak. He spoke through an Igbo man, although his dialect was different. Many people laughed at the way he used words strangely. Instead of saying "myself," he always said, "my buttocks." But he was a man of commanding presence. He said he was one of them, as they could see.

The white man was also their brother because they were all sons of God. He told them about this new God, the Creator of all the world and of men and women. He told them they worshipped false gods. A deep murmur went through the crowd when he said this. He told them that when men died they went before the true God for judgment. Those who bowed to false gods were thrown into a fire. But men who worshipped the true God lived forever in His happy kingdom.

"Your buttocks understand our language," said someone lightheartedly, and the crowd laughed.

"What did he say?" the white man asked the interpreter. Before he could answer, another man asked a question:

"Where is the white man's horse?" The Igbo missionaries decided he probably meant his bicycle. They told the white man, and he smiled kindly.

"Tell them that I shall bring many iron horses when we have settled down among them. Some of them will even ride an iron horse themselves." Few heard this. They were talking excitedly because the white man had said he was going to live among them. They had not thought about that.

An old man asked, "Which is this god of yours, the goddess of the earth, the god of the sky, or what?"

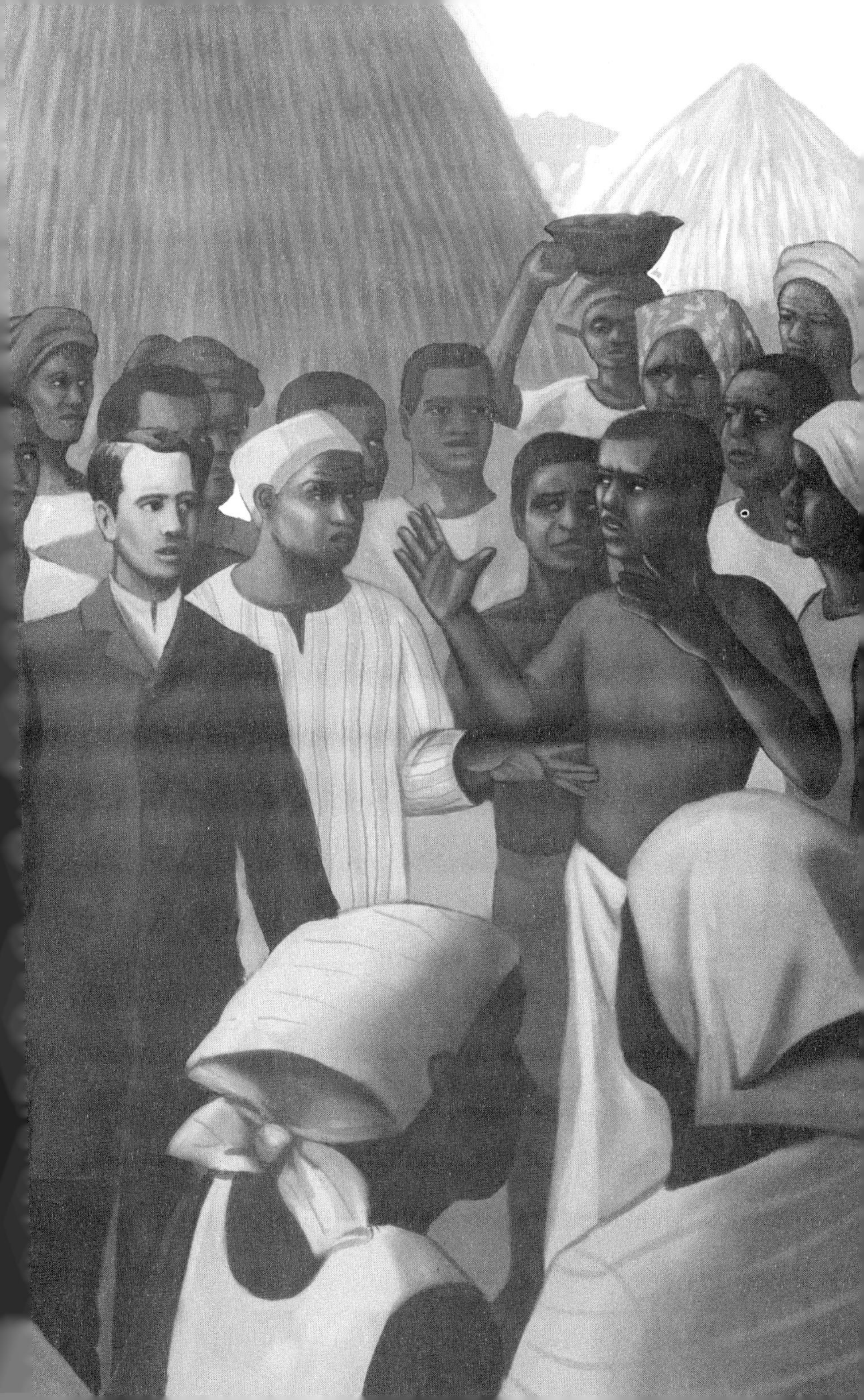

The white man answered, "All the gods you named are not gods at all. They are gods of deceit who tell you to kill your fellows and destroy innocent children. There is only one true God."

"If we leave our gods, who will protect us from the anger of our neglected gods and ancestors?"

"Your gods are not alive and cannot do you any harm," said the white man. "They are pieces of wood and stone."

When this was interpreted, the men of Mbanta broke into laughter. These men must be mad, they said to themselves. How else could they say that Ani was harmless? Some of the men began to go away.

Then the missionaries burst into song. It was a rollicking song that could pluck at silent chords in the heart of an Igbo man. The interpreter explained each verse to the audience, many of whom now stood enthralled. It was a story of brothers who lived in fear, ignorant of the love of God.

After the singing, the interpreter spoke about the Son of God, Jesu Kristi. Okonkwo, who had only stayed in the hope that it might come to chasing the men out of the village or whipping them, said:

"You told us there was only one god. Now you talk about his son. He must have a wife, then."

"I did not say he had a son," said the interpreter, somewhat lamely. The missionary went on to talk about the Holy Trinity. At the end, Okonkwo was convinced the man was mad. He shrugged his shoulders and went away.

There was a young lad who had been captivated by the missionary's talk. His name was Nwoye. It was not the mad logic of the Trinity that captivated him. It was the poetry of the new religion. The hymn about the brothers who sat in fear seemed to answer some vague questions he had—the question of the twins crying in the bush and the question of Ikemefuna who was killed. He felt a relief as the hymn poured into his parched soul. The words of the hymn were like drops of frozen rain melting on the dry, panting earth. Nwoye's immature mind was greatly puzzled.

Chapter 17

The missionaries spent their first four nights in the marketplace, then they went into the village to preach the gospel. They asked who the king was, and they were told there was no king. "We have men of high title and the chief priests and elders," the people of the village said.

It was not easy getting the men of high title and the elders together. In the end, the missionaries were received by the elders of Mbanta. They asked for a plot of land to build their church.

Every village had its "evil forest." In it were buried those who died of evil diseases like leprosy and smallpox. It was also the dumping ground for potent charms of great medicine men when they died. The "evil forest" was alive with sinister forces. It was such a forest that the rulers of Mbanta gave to the missionaries. They did not want them, so they made an offer nobody in his senses would accept.

"They boast about their victory over death. Let us give them a real battlefield in which to show their victory," said Uchendu. The elders laughed and agreed, and they offered the missionaries as much of the Evil Forest as they cared to take. To their amazement, the missionaries thanked them and burst into song.

"They do not understand," said some of the elders. "But they will understand when they go to their plot of land tomorrow morning."

The next morning, the crazy men began to clear a part of the forest and build their house. The people of Mbanta expected them to be dead in four days. Four days passed, and none of them died. Everyone was puzzled. It became known that the white man's magic was unbelievably powerful. Not long after, he won his first three converts.

Although Nwoye had been attracted to the new faith from the first day, he kept it secret. He dared not go too close to the missionaries for fear of his father. But when they preached in the marketplace, Nwoye was there.

"We have now built a church," said Mr. Kiaga, the interpreter, "and we want you to come in every seventh day to worship the true God." The following Sunday, Nwoye passed and repassed the little red-earth and thatch building without finding the courage to enter. He heard singing that was loud and confident. Nwoye finally returned home.

It was well-known in Mbanta that their gods would sometimes deliberately allow a man to go on defying them. Even in such cases, they only allowed twenty-eight days. Beyond that limit, no man could go. So excitement mounted in the village. The villagers were so certain about the doom that awaited the missionaries that one or two converts thought it wise to suspend their faith in the new god.

At last, the day came by which the missionaries should have died. But they were still alive, building a new house for their teacher, Mr. Kiaga. That week they won a handful more converts. For the first time, they had a woman, Nneka, the wife of Amadi, a prosperous farmer. She was about to give birth.

Nneka had had four previous pregnancies and childbirths. Each time she had borne twins, and they had been immediately thrown away. Her husband and his family were already becoming highly critical of such a woman and were not upset when she fled to join the Christians. It was good riddance.

One morning, Okonkwo's cousin, Amikwu, was passing by the church on his way home from the next village when he saw Nwoye among the Christians. He was greatly surprised. When he got home, he went straight to Okonkwo's hut and told him. Okonkwo sat unmoved.

It was late afternoon before Nwoye returned. He went into his father's hut and saluted him, but Okonkwo did not answer. Nwoye turned to leave when his father, suddenly overcome with fury, sprang to his feet and gripped him by the neck.

"Where have you been?" he stammered.

Nwoye struggled to free himself.

"Answer me," roared Okonkwo, "before I kill you!" He seized a heavy stick and hit him.

"Answer me!" he roared again. Nwoye stood looking at him and did not say a word. The women were screaming outside, afraid to go in.

"Leave that boy at once!" said a voice. It was Okonkwo's uncle, Uchendu. "Are you mad?"

Okonkwo did not answer. But he let go of Nwoye, who walked away and never returned.

He went back to the church and told Mr. Kiaga that he had decided to go to Umuofia where the white missionary had set up a school to teach young Christians to read and write.

Mr. Kiaga's joy was very great. "Blessed is he who forsakes his father and mother for my sake," he said.

Nwoye did not fully understand, but he was happy to leave his father. He would return later to his mother and his siblings and convert them.

As Okonkwo sat in his hut that night, a sudden fury rose within him, and he felt a strong desire to take his machete and wipe out the church. But, he told himself that Nwoye was not worth fighting for. Why should he be cursed with such a son? Suppose when he died all his male children decided to follow Nwoye's steps? Okonkwo felt a cold shudder as he saw himself and his fathers crowding around their ancestral shrine waiting in vain for worship and finding nothing but the ashes of bygone days.

Okonkwo was once called the "Roaring Flame." As he looked into the log fire, he recalled the name. He was a flaming fire. How could he have begotten such a son as Nwoye? But Nwoye resembled his grandfather. He pushed the thought out of his mind.

He sighed heavily, and as if in sympathy the fire also sighed. Then Okonkwo's eyes were opened. Living fire begets cold ash. He sighed again, deeply.

Chapter 18

The young church in Mbanta had a few crises. At first, the clan had assumed it would not survive. But it had gone on. The clan was not overly worried. If a gang of *efulefu* decided to live in the Evil Forest, it was their own affair. The Evil Forest was a fit home for them. It was true they were rescuing twins, but they never brought them into the village. Surely, the earth goddess would not visit the sins of the missionaries on the innocent villagers.

On one occasion, the missionaries had tried to overstep their bounds. Three converts had gone into the village and said they would burn all the shrines. The villagers seized and beat them.

But stories were gaining ground that the missionaries had also brought a government. It was said they had built a place of judgment in Umuofia to protect the followers of their religion. It was even said they had hanged a man who had killed a missionary.

In Mbanta, these stories seemed like fairy tales. Mr. Kiaga was quite harmless. No one could kill his converts, for they still belonged to the clan. The little church was too deeply involved in its own troubles to annoy the clan. It began with the question of admitting outcasts.

The *osu,*[27] thought it was possible they would be received. One Sunday, two went into the church. There was a stir, but so great was the work the new religion had done that the others did not immediately leave when the outcasts entered. After the service, the whole church raised a protest and the people were about to drive the *osu* out when Mr. Kiaga stopped them. "We are all children of God. We must receive our brothers," he said.

"You do not understand," said one convert. "This is a matter of which we know." And he told him what an *osu* was.

The *osu* was a person dedicated to a god, set apart forever, and his children after him. He could neither marry nor be married. He was an outcast. Wherever he went, he carried the mark with him—long, tangled, and dirty hair. A razor was forbidden. An *osu* could not attend a meeting of the free-born. When he died, he was buried in the Evil Forest. How could such a man be a follower of Christ?

---

27. *osu* outcast

"He needs Christ more than you and I," said Mr. Kiaga.

"Then I shall go back to the clan," said the convert. He went. Mr. Kiaga stood firm, and it was his firmness that saved the church. The wavering converts took strength from him. He ordered the outcasts to shave their hair. At first, they were afraid they might die.

"The heathen also said I would die if I built my church on this ground. Am I dead? The heathen speak falsehoods. Only the word of God is true."

Soon the outcasts were the strongest members of the new faith. Nearly all the *osu* in Mbanta joined the church. One of them brought the church into serious conflict with the clan a year later by killing the sacred python, the most revered animal. If someone from the clan killed a python accidentally, he made sacrifices and performed an expensive burial ceremony.

Perhaps the *osu* did not kill the python. That was the way the clan first looked at it. The story had arisen among the Christians. All the same, the elders had to decide on an action. Many spoke at great length. Okonkwo, who had begun to take a part in village affairs, said the gang should be chased from the village or there would be no peace.

Others, though, prevailed. "It is not our custom to fight for our gods," said one. "Let us not start now."

"These people are daily pouring filth over us, and Okeke says we should pretend not to see." Okonkwo made a sound of disgust. Such a thing would never happen in his fatherland, Umuofia, he thought.

In the end, it was decided to ignore the Christians. Okonkwo ground his teeth in disgust.

That night a bell-man went through Mbanta proclaiming that members of the church were now excluded from the life of the clan. The next day, when some women set out to the stream, and others to the village earth-pit, they were chased away.

"What does it all mean?" asked Mr. Kiaga.

"The village has outlawed us," said a woman. Some men wanted to fight the villagers, but Mr. Kiaga restrained them. He wanted to know why they had been outlawed.

"They say Okoli killed the sacred python," said one.

"It is false," said another. "Okoki told me himself."

Okoli was not there to answer. He had fallen ill and died the previous night. His death showed that the gods were still able to fight their own battles. The clan saw no reason then to molest the Christians.

Chapter 19

It was going to be Okonkwo's last harvest in Mbanta. The seven wasted and weary years were at last dragging to a close. Although he had prospered in his motherland, Okonkwo knew he would have prospered more in Umuofia, in the land of his fathers. His mother's kin had been very kind to him, and he was grateful. He had called his first child born in exile Nneka—"Mother is Supreme"—out of politeness to his mother's kinsmen. However, two years later when a son was born, he called him Nwofia—"Born in the Wilderness."

As soon as he entered his last year in exile, Okonkwo sent money to Obierika to build him two huts where he and his family would live. He could not ask another man to build his hut. Those things a man built for himself.

As the last heavy rains of the year began to fall, Obierika sent word that the huts had been built. Okonkwo waited impatiently for the dry season to come. Finally, the rain became lighter and lighter. Okonkwo called his three wives and told them to get things together for a great feast. "I must thank my mother's kinsmen before I go," he said.

Ekwefi would provide cassava. Nwoye's mother and Ojiugo would provide the smoked fish, palm-oil, and pepper. Okonkwo would bring meat and yams.

Okonkwo was thorough in everything he did. When his wife Ekwefi protested that two goats were sufficient for the feast, he told her that it was not her affair.

"I am calling a feast because my mother's people have been good to me. I must show my gratitude."

Three goats and a number of fowls were slaughtered. It was like a wedding feast. All the kinsmen were invited to the feast. The oldest member of the family was Okonkwo's uncle, Uchendu. The kola nut was given him to break, and he prayed to the ancestors. He asked them for health and children. "We do not ask for wealth because he who has health and children will also have wealth." He prayed especially for Okonkwo and his family.

As the broken kola nuts were passed around, Okonkwo's wives and children began to bring out the food. There was so much food and drink that many kinsmen whistled in surprise. When all was laid out, Okonkwo rose to speak.

"I beg you to accept this little kola," he said. "It is not to pay you back for all you did for me in these seven years. A child cannot pay for its mother's milk. I have only called you together because it is good for kinsmen to meet."

Yam stew was served first, then *foo-foo* and melon seed soup and bitter-leaf soup. The meat was shared so that everyone had a portion. As the wine was drunk, one of the kinsmen rose to thank Okonkwo.

"If I say that we did not expect such a big feast, it would be suggesting we did not know how open-handed our son, Okonkwo, is. We all know him, and we expected a big feast but it turned out even bigger than we expected. Thank you. May all you took out return tenfold. A man who calls his kinsmen to a feast does not do so to save them from starving. We come together because it is good for kinsmen to do so. You may ask why I am saying this. I say it because I fear for the younger generation, for you people. I have only a short time to live. But I fear for you young people because you do not understand how strong the bond of kinship is. You do not know how to speak with one voice. What is the result? An evil religion has settled among you. A man can now leave his father and brothers. He can curse the gods of his father and his ancestors like a hunter's dog that suddenly turns on its master. I fear for you; I fear for the clan." He turned again to Okonkwo and said, "Thank you for calling us together."

Part 3 Return to Umuofia

Chapter 20

Seven years was a long time to be away from one's clan. A man's place was not always there, waiting for him. As soon as he left, someone else rose to fill it.

Okonkwo knew these things. He knew he had lost his place among the nine masked spirits who administered justice in the clan. He had lost the chance to lead his warlike clan against the new religion. He had lost the years in which he might have taken the highest titles. But he was determined his return should be marked by his people. He would regain the seven wasted years.

The first thing he would do would be to rebuild his compound on a more magnificent scale. He would build huts for two new wives. Then he would show his wealth by initiating his sons into the *ozo*[28] society. Only the great men in the clan did this. Okonkwo saw himself taking the highest title in the land.

As the years had passed, it had seemed to him that his *chi* might be making amends for the past disaster. His yams grew abundantly both in his motherland and in Umuofia. Then the tragedy of his first son had occurred. At first, it appeared as if it might prove too great for his spirit. In the end, Okonkwo overcame his sorrow. He had five other sons.

He sent for his sons. The youngest was four. "You have all seen the great abomination of your brother. I will only have a son who is a man. If any of you prefers to be a woman, let him follow Nwoye while I am alive so I can curse him."

---

28. *ozo* the name of one of the titles or ranks in Igbo society

Okonkwo was very lucky in his daughters. He never stopped regretting Ezinma was a girl. She alone understood his every mood. A bond of sympathy had grown between them as the years had passed.

Ezinma became one of the most beautiful girls in Mbanta. She was called Crystal of Beauty, as her mother had been called in her youth. The young ailing girl had grown, almost overnight, into a healthy maiden. She had her moments when she snapped at everybody like an angry dog. As long as these moods lasted, she could bear no other person but her father.

Many young men and prosperous middle-aged men of Mbanta wanted to marry her. She refused them all, because her father had said to her, "There are many good people here, but I shall be happy if you marry in Umuofia when we return home."

That was all he said, but Ezinma had seen clearly the thought behind the few words. She had agreed. She also agreed to explain to Obiageli, her half-sister. Ezinma wielded a strong influence over her half-sister, and she agreed also. The two of them refused every offer of marriage in Mbanta.

"I wish she were a boy," Okonkwo thought. Who else among his children could have read his thoughts so well? With two beautiful grown-up daughters, his return to Umuofia would attract considerable attention. His future sons-in-law would be men of authority. The poor would not dare come forth.

Umuofia had indeed changed. The church had come and led many astray. Sometimes a worthy man had joined. Such a man was Ogbuefi Ugonna, who had taken two titles and, like a madman, had cut the anklet of his titles and cast it away to join the church.

Apart from the church, the white men had also brought a government. They had built a court where the District Commissioner judged cases in ignorance. He had court messengers who brought men before him. Many of these messengers came from Umuru, where the white men first had come many years before. These court messengers guarded the prison, which was full of men who had offended against the white men's law. Some had thrown away their twins, and some had molested the Christians. They were beaten in the prison and had to work every morning cleaning the government compound and fetching wood.

Okonkwo's head was bowed in sadness as Obierika told him these things.

"I cannot understand these things you tell me. What has happened to our people? Why have they lost the power to fight?"

"Our own men and sons have joined the ranks of the stranger," said Obierika. "We would find it easy to drive out the white men in Umuofia, but people would go to Umuru and bring the soldiers, and we would be like Abame. The white man is very clever. He came quietly with his religion. We were amused and allowed him to stay. Now, he has won our brothers, and our clan can no longer act like one. He has put a knife on the things that held us together and we have fallen apart."

The two men sat in silence for a long while afterwards.

Chapter 21

Many in Umuofia did not feel as strongly as Okonkwo about the white man. Indeed the white man had brought a lunatic religion. But he had also built a trading post and, for the first time, palm-oil had become a thing of great price and money flowed in Umuofia.

Even in the matter of religion, feelings were changing. This change was because of Mr. Brown, a white missionary, who was firm about restraining his flock from enraging the clan. He came to be respected even by the clan. He made friends with some of the great men of the clan. One of the great men in a neighboring village was called Akunna, and he had given one of his sons to be taught at Mr. Brown's school. Mr. Brown and Akunna spent long hours talking about religion. Neither converted the other but they learned more about their different beliefs.

"We believe in one God and call him Chukwu. He made the world and all the other gods," said Akunna.

"There are no other gods," Mr. Brown said. "You carve wood and call it a god. But it is still wood."

"Yes," said Akunna, "but it was made by Chukwu. He made it for his messengers so we could approach Him through them. It is like you. You are the head of your church."

Mr. Brown protested that the head was God.

"I know," said Akunna, "but somebody like yourself must be the head here. We approach Chukwu through his servants. If they fail, we go to the last source of hope. We appear to pay greater attention to the little gods, but that is not so. We worry them more because we do not want to worry their master."

In this way, Mr. Brown learned a good deal about the religion of the clan and decided an attack on it would not succeed. He decided to build a school and a little hospital in Umuofia. He went from family to family begging people to send their children to his school. He said that leaders of the land in the future would be men and women who could read and write.

In the end, Mr. Brown's arguments had an effect. More people came to the school. They were not all young. They worked on their farms in the morning and went to school in the afternoon. It was not long before people began to say that the white man's medicine was quickly working. A few months in the school was enough to make one a court messenger or even a court clerk. Those who stayed longer became teachers. New churches were established in the surrounding villages and a few schools with them. But Mr. Brown's health was breaking down. In the end, he had to leave his flock, sad and broken.

It was the first rainy season after Okonkwo's return that Mr. Brown left for home. As soon as he had heard of Okonkwo's return, Mr. Brown paid him a visit. Nwoye was now at the training college for teachers in Umuru. Mr. Brown had hoped that Okonkwo would be happy to hear it. But Okonkwo had driven Mr. Brown away with the threat that if he entered the compound again, he would be carried out of it.

Okonkwo's return was not as memorable as he had wished. It was true his beautiful daughters aroused great interest, and marriage negotiations were soon underway, but beyond that, Umuofia took little notice. The clan had changed so much that it was barely recognizable. The new religion and government and trading stores were very much on everyone's mind. Some saw them as evil, but even they talked of little else. They certainly had not spoken of Okonkwo's return.

It was the wrong year, too. If Okonkwo had immediately initiated his sons into the *ozo* society as he had planned, it would have caused a stir. But the rite was only performed once every three years.

Okonkwo was deeply grieved. It was not just personal. He mourned for the clan, which he saw breaking up and falling apart, and he mourned for the warlike men of Umuofia, who had become soft like women.

Chapter 22

Mr. Brown's successor[29] was the Reverend James Smith, and he was a different kind of man. He saw things as either good or evil. Mr. Smith was distressed by how little the flock knew about even such things as the Sacraments. Mr. Brown had thought of nothing but numbers. He should have known the kingdom of God did not depend on crowds.

Within a few weeks of his arrival, Mr. Smith had suspended a young woman from the church. She had allowed her heathen husband to mutilate her dead child. The child had been declared an *ogbanje*. Mr. Smith was filled with wrath when he heard of this. He did not believe the story that even some of the most faithful told about these evil children.

The overly enthusiastic converts who had disliked Mr. Brown's restraint now were in favor. One, Enoch, had a faith so much greater than Mr. Brown's that the villagers called him the outsider who wept louder than the bereaved.

Enoch was short and slight, and he always seemed to be in a hurry. Such was the energy in

---

29. successor one that comes after another, as to an office

Enoch's small body that it was always involved in quarrels and fights. It was Enoch who started the great conflict between church and clan in Umuofia that had been gathering since Mr. Brown had left.

It happened during the annual ceremony for the earth goddess. One of the greatest crimes a man could commit was to unmask an *egwugwu* in public. This is what Enoch did.

The annual worship happened on a Sunday, and the masked spirits were abroad. Therefore, Christian women who had been to church could not go home. Some of their men had gone out to beg the *egwugwu* to retire and let the women pass. They agreed and were already leaving when Enoch boasted they would not dare touch a Christian. They all came back and one of them gave Enoch a good stroke with the cane he carried. Enoch fell on him and tore off his mask. The other *egwugwu* surrounded their desecrated[30] companion and led him away. Enoch had killed an ancestral spirit, and Umuofia was in confusion.

That night the Mother of the Spirits walked the clan, weeping for her murdered son. Not even the oldest man in Umuofia had ever heard such a strange and fearful sound, and it was never to be heard again. It seemed as if the very soul of the tribe wept for a great evil that was coming—its own death.

The next day all the *egwugwu* of Umuofia assembled. It was a terrible gathering. From the marketplace, the furious band made for Enoch's compound. Some of the elders of the clan went with them. Others listened from the safety of their huts.

The leaders of the Christians had met at Mr. Smith's house the night before. They could hear the Mother of Spirits wailing for her son. The chilling

---

30. desecrated unfit for ceremonial use, unholy

sound affected Mr. Smith, and for the first time he seemed to be afraid.

"What are they planning to do?" he asked. No one knew. Such a thing had never happened. "We cannot offer resistance. Our strength lies in the Lord." They knelt and prayed and decided to hide Enoch.

The band of *egwugwu* moved furiously to Enoch's compound and burned it to the ground. From there they made for the church, ready for destruction.

Mr. Smith was in the church when he heard them coming. When he saw the first few *egwugwu,* he nearly ran away. He overcame this impulse and instead walked toward the approaching spirits.

They surged forward, and the bamboo fence gave way. Bells clanged, machetes clashed, and the air was full of dust and weird sounds. Mr. Smith heard footsteps behind him. It was Okeke, his interpreter. Okeke had strongly condemned Enoch's behavior. Mr. Smith had scolded him. Now, as he stood by Mr. Smith and faced the angry spirits, the preacher gave him a wan[31] smile.

For a moment, the onrush of the *egwugwu* was stopped by the two men silently standing. Then the second onrush swallowed up the two men. A voice rose above the sounds, and there was silence.

Ajofia began to speak. He was the leading *egwugwu.* His voice was unmistakable. He dug his rattling spear into the ground and addressed the interpreter. "Tell the white man we will not do him harm. Tell him to return to his house. We liked his brother who was here before, and for his sake we will not harm his brother. But this shrine he built must be destroyed. You can stay with us if you like our ways. You can worship your own god. Our anger is great but we have held it down so we can talk to you."

---

31. wan weak

"Tell them to go away," Mr. Smith told his interpreter. "This is the house of God. I will not live to see it desecrated."

Okeke interpreted wisely. "The white man says he is happy you have come to him with your grievances, like friends. He asks you leave the matter in his hands."

"We cannot. He does not understand our customs, just as we do not understand his. Let him go away."

Mr. Smith stood his ground. But he could not save his church. When the *egwugwu* went away the church was a pile of ashes. For the moment, the spirit of the clan was at peace.

Chapter 23

For the first time in many years, Okonkwo had a feeling like happiness. The clan that had turned false on him appeared to be making amends.

He had spoken violently to his clansmen when they had met to decide on their actions. They had listened to him with respect. Although they had not agreed to kill the missionary or drive away the Christians, they had agreed to do something substantial. And they had done it.

For two days after the destruction of the church, nothing happened. Every man in Umuofia was armed with a gun or a machete. They would not be caught unawares, like the men of Abame.

Then the District Commissioner returned. Mr. Smith went to him and they had a long talk. Three days later, the Commissioner sent his messenger asking the leaders to meet him in his headquarters. Okonkwo was among the six leaders he invited.

Okonkwo warned the others to be fully armed. "We must be prepared," he said.

The six men went to see the District Commissioner armed with machetes. They did not carry guns, as that would be unseemly. The Commissioner received them politely. They put their goatskin bags and machetes on the floor and sat.

"I asked you to come because of what happened. Let us talk about it like friends and find a way of ensuring it does not happen again," said the Commissioner.

Ogbuefi Ekwueme rose and began to tell the story.

"Wait a minute," said the Commissioner. "I want to bring in my men so they too can hear." The interpreter left and returned with twelve men. They sat with the men of Umuofia, and Ogbuefi began to tell the story of what Enoch had done.

It happened so fast the six men did not see it coming. There was only a brief scuffle. The six men were handcuffed and led into the guardroom.

"We will not do you any harm," the Commissioner said to them later, "if you cooperate. We have brought a peaceful administration so you may be happy. If any man ill-treats you, we will come to your rescue, but we will not allow you to ill-treat others. You burned people's houses and their church. I have decided you will pay a fine of two hundred bags of cowries. When you agree, I will release you."

The six men were sullen and silent. As soon as the Commissioner left, the head messenger shaved off all the hair on their heads. The six men ate nothing throughout that day and the next. They were given no water to drink. At night, the messengers came to laugh at them and knock their heads together.

The men found no words to speak. On the third day, when they could no longer bear the hunger and the insults, they began to talk of giving in.

"We should have killed the white man," Okonkwo snarled.

"Who wants to kill the white man?" asked a messenger who came in. He carried a strong stick and hit each man. Okonkwo was choked with hate.

When the men were locked up, messengers went to Umuofia to tell the people the men would not be released until the fine was paid, and if it were not, the men would be hanged. The news traveled quickly through the villages, expanding as it went. Some said the soldiers were already on their way to shoot the people of Umuofia, as they had in Abame.

Umuofia was like a startled animal with its ears erect, sniffing the silent air and not knowing which way to run. The silence was broken by the village crier, who called the men in Umuofia to meet the next morning.

At the meeting, the men of Umuofia decided to collect the two hundred and fifty bags of cowries. They did not know that fifty bags would go to the court messengers, who had increased the fine.

Chapter 24

Okonkwo and his fellow prisoners were set free when the fine was paid. The District Commissioner spoke to them again about peace and good government. The men did not listen. They just sat. In the end, they were told to go home. They rose and spoke to no one.

On the way back to the village, the six men met women and children going to the stream with their waterpots. The men wore such fearsome expressions that the women said nothing, but edged out of the way. In the village, little groups of men joined them until they became a sizable community. The village was astir in a silent, subdued way.

Ezinma had prepared food for her father. He ate it absentmindedly, to please her. Obierika urged him to eat. Nobody else spoke, but they noticed the long stripes on Okonkwo's back where the whip had cut him.

The village crier announced another meeting for the next morning. Everyone knew Umuofia was at last going to speak about what was happening.

Okonkwo slept little that night. The bitterness in his heart was now mixed with childlike excitement. Before he went to bed, he took down his war dress. It was satisfactory, he thought.

He lay on his bed and thought about his treatment in the white man's court, and he swore vengeance. If Umuofia decided on war, all would be well. If the villagers chose to be cowards, he would avenge himself. "Worthy men are no more," he sighed, remembering days of war.

The marketplace began to fill when the sun rose. Obierika was waiting when Okonkwo came and called him. When Okonkwo and Obierika got to the meeting place, there were already so many people that if one threw a grain of sand it would not find its way to earth again. Many more people were coming.

It warmed Okonkwo's heart to see such strength of numbers.

Onyeka used his booming voice to establish silence in his welcome of the clan. Okika, one of the six who had been imprisoned, began to speak:

"You all know why we are here, when we should be building our barns or mending our huts. This is a great gathering. But are we all here? Are all the sons of Umuofia here? They are not. They have broken the clan and gone their separate ways. If we fight the stranger, we shall hit our brothers. But we must do it. Our fathers never dreamed of such a thing, but a white man never came to them. We must root out this evil. If our brothers take the side of evil, we must root them out, too. We must do it now. We must bail this water now when it is only ankle-deep."

At this point, there was a sudden stir in the crowd. There was a sharp bend in the road that led to the marketplace. No one had seen the approach of the five court messengers until they came around the bend a few paces from the edge of the crowd. Okonkwo was sitting at the edge.

He sprang to his feet as soon as he saw who it was. He confronted the head messenger, trembling with hate, unable to say a word. The man was fearless and stood his ground, his four men behind him.

In that brief moment, the world seemed to stand still, waiting. There was utter silence. The men of Umuofia waited, merged into the backdrop of trees.

The spell was broken by the head messenger. "Let me pass," he ordered.

"What do you want here?"

"The white man whose power you know too well has ordered this meeting to stop."

In a flash, Okonkwo drew his machete. The messenger crouched to avoid the blow. It was useless. Okonkwo's machete descended twice and the man's head lay beside his uniformed body.

The waiting crowd jumped to life and the meeting was stopped. Okonkwo stood looking at the dead man. He knew that Umuofia would not go to war. He knew because they had let the other messengers escape. They broke into turmoil instead of action. He felt the fright of the people in the turmoil. He heard voices asking, "Why did he do it?"

He wiped his machete on the sand and went away.

Chapter 25

When the District Commissioner arrived at Okonkwo's compound at the head of an armed band of soldiers, he found a small crowd of men sitting wearily in Okonkwo's hut. He commanded them to come outside, and they obeyed without a murmur.

"Which among you is Okonkwo?" he asked through his interpreter.

"He is not here," replied Obierika.

"Where is he?"

"He is not here!"

The Commissioner became angry and red in the face. He warned the men that if they did not produce Okonkwo, he would lock them all up.

Obierika spoke again. "We can take you where he is, and perhaps your men will help us."

The Commissioner did not understand. One of the most infuriating habits of these people was their love of extra words, he thought.

Obierika with five or six others led the way. The Commissioner and his men followed. He had warned Obierika that if he and his men played any monkey tricks, they would be shot and so they went.

There was a small bush behind Okonkwo's compound. It was to this bush that Obierika went.

Then they came to the tree from which Okonkwo's body was dangling, and they stopped.

"Perhaps your men can help us bring him down and bury him," Obierika said. "We have sent for strangers from another village to do it, but they may be a long time coming."

The Commissioner changed from a businesslike administrator to a student of primitive customs.

"Why can't you take him down yourselves?"

"It is against our custom," said one of the men. "It is an abomination for a man to take his own life. It is an offense against the Earth, and a man who commits it will not be buried by his clansmen. His body is evil, and only strangers may touch it. That is why we ask your people, because you are strangers."

"Will you bury him like any other man?" asked the Commissioner.

"We cannot bury him. Only strangers can. We shall pay your men to do it. When he has been buried, we will then do our duty by him. We will make sacrifices to cleanse the desecrated land."

Obierika, who had been gazing steadily at his friend's dangling body, turned suddenly to the District Commissioner and said fiercely, "That man was one of the greatest men in Umuofia. You drove him to kill himself, and now he will be buried like a dog. . . ." He could not say any more. His voice trembled and choked his words.

"Take down the body," the Commissioner ordered his chief messenger, "and bring it and all these people to the court."

"Yes, sah," the messenger said, saluting.

The Commissioner went away, taking three of the soldiers with him. In the many years in which he had toiled to bring civilization to different parts of Africa, the Commissioner had learned a number of things. One was that a District Commissioner must never attend to such undignified details as cutting a hanged man from a tree. Such attention would give the natives a poor opinion of him. In the book he planned to write, he would stress that point.

As he walked back to the court, he thought about that book. Every day brought new material. The story of this man who had killed a messenger and hanged himself would make interesting reading. One could almost write a whole chapter on him or at least a reasonable paragraph. There was so much else to include, and one must be firm in cutting out details. He had already chosen the title of the book, after much thought: *The Pacification of the Primitive Tribes of the Lower Niger.*

GLOSSARY

agbala a woman, also used to refer to a man with no title

chi personal god

efulefu worthless man

egwugwu a man who impersonates one of the ancestral spirits of the village

ekwe a musical instrument; a type of drum made of wood

foo-foo a dough made from mashed yams

fronds palm leaves

iyi-uwa a special kind of stone that links the ogbanje and the spirit world, only if the *iyi-uwa* is discovered and destroyed, will the child live

kola nut a nut inside the kola; it is sectional like a grapefruit

ogbanje a child who repeatedly dies and returns to his or her mother to be reborn.

osu outcast

ozo the name of one of the titles or ranks in Igbo society

uri part of the engagement ceremony when the dowry, or bride-price, is paid

REVIEWING YOUR READING

CHAPTERS 1–4

FINDING THE MAIN IDEA

1. Chapter 3 is mainly about

(A) how Okonkwo disliked his father.

(B) the conflict between Okonkwo and his father.

(C) how Okonkwo's father, Unoka, failed as a farmer.

(D) how Okonkwo worked as a young man to build his fortune.

REMEMBERING DETAILS

2. What is Okonkwo's relationship with Ikemefuna like?

(A) They do not get along.

(B) Okonkwo favors Ikemefuna over Nwoye.

(C) Okonkwo only shows anger toward Ikemefuna.

(D) They were like father and son.

DRAWING CONCLUSIONS

3. You can conclude that the reason Okonkwo rules his household sternly is

(A) he is afraid of seeming weak like his father.

(B) he has been taught by his father that it is important to rule the household that way.

(C) the men he admires run their households with a heavy hand.

(D) both A and C.

IDENTIFYING THE MOOD

4. At the village meeting in Chapter 2, the mood of the crowd is

(A) proud.

(B) timid.

(C) happy.

(D) angry.

CRITICAL THINKING

5. Comprehension Why did Mbaino decide to offer a young boy and girl to Umuofia rather than go to war?

6. Analysis Explain how Unoka's *chi* affected his life.

7. Compare and Contrast Describe how Okonkwo and his father are alike and how they differ.

CHAPTERS 5–8

FINDING THE MAIN IDEA

1. Chapters 5 and 6 are mainly about

(A) the two-day Feast of the New Yam.

(B) the wrestling during the festival.

(C) how Ikemefuna came to Okonkwo's household.

(D) daily life in Okonkwo's household.

REMEMBERING DETAILS

2. How has Nwoye begun to "act like a man"?

(A) He enjoys listening to the story about the earth and the sky.

(B) He spends less time with Ikemefuna.

(C) He listens to stories about tribal wars.

(D) He goes to collect firewood.

DRAWING CONCLUSIONS

3. Nwoye grumbles at having to help his mother because

(A) he is lazy.

(B) he has been taught to do that by Ikemefuna.

(C) he wants to be a grown-up and please his father.

(D) A and C.

IDENTIFYING THE MOOD

4. When the locusts descend, the mood of the village is

(A) terrified.

(B) joyful.

(C) panicked.

(D) bewildered.

CRITICAL THINKING

5. Description Explain the process by which Okonkwo's family gets ready for the Feast of the New Yam.

6. Analysis Explain why Okonkwo killed Ikemefuna.

7. Analysis Explain why Okonkwo mentions the killing to his friend Obierika.

CHAPTERS 9–11

FINDING THE MAIN IDEA

1. Chapter 11 is mainly about

(A) Ezinma's special place in the clan.

(B) Okonkwo's frantic attempt to follow Ezinma.

(C) the journey Ezinma took with Chielo.

(D) the concern Ezinma's parents have for her.

REMEMBERING DETAILS

2. To help cure Ezinma's fever, Okonkwo

(A) consults with Chielo.

(B) collects barks, grasses, and leaves for medicine.

(C) prays to the gods.

(D) asks the medicine man to visit.

DRAWING CONCLUSIONS

3. Okonkwo comes to the shrine to find Ezinma and Chielo because

(A) he wants to prove that Ekwefi is frightened for no reason.

(B) he is concerned himself, although he will not admit it.

(C) he wants to make sure Ekwefi will not anger the priestess.

(D) he is trying to find Ezinma and Ekwefi.

IDENTIFYING THE MOOD

4. As Ekwefi follows Chielo and Ezinma, her mood is

(A) defiant.

(B) determined.

(C) frightened.

(D) angry.

CRITICAL THINKING

5. **Summary** Describe how the medicine man found Ezinma's *iyi-uwa.*

6. **Comprehension** Explain why the *egwugwu* decided to rule in favor of Mgbafo and her family.

7. **Comprehension** Explain why Ezinma is so precious to her mother.

CHAPTERS 12–15

FINDING THE MAIN IDEA

1. Chapters 14 and 15 are mainly about

(A) the differences between Mbanta and Umuofia.

(B) Okonkwo's bad *chi.*

(C) how Okonkwo plans to regain his position in his village.

(D) Okonkwo's life in exile.

REMEMBERING DETAILS

2. Okonkwo's killing of his kinsman is considered a "female" crime because

(A) the victim was from his mother's side of the family.

(B) the victim was young and not yet a man.

(C) Okonkwo did not mean to kill him.

(D) Okonkwo used a gun rather than his hands.

DRAWING CONCLUSIONS

3. Uchendu gathers his family and Okonkwo and talks to them because

(A) he wants to imply to Okonkwo that he is being disrespectful of his mother's clan.

(B) he wants to tell Okonkwo that he should not feel sorry for himself.

(C) he wants to prove to Okonkwo that his mother's village is superior to Umuofia.

(D) both A and B.

IDENTIFYING THE MOOD

4. As he begins his farming in Mbanta, Okonkwo's mood is one of

(A) hope.

(B) despair.

(C) rage.

(D) thankfulness.

CRITICAL THINKING

5. **Comprehension** Explain the duties of the *egwugwu.*

6. **Comprehension** Why did Obierika, Okonkwo's friend, come to his compound and help destroy it?

7. **Summarize** Explain the events that led to the destruction of Abame.

CHAPTERS 16–19

FINDING THE MAIN IDEA

1. Chapters 16–18 are mainly about

(A) how Nwoye became a convert to the new religion.

(B) how the Christians changed Igbo society.

(C) how the Christian church developed in Mbanta.

(D) how the Christian church developed in Umuofia.

REMEMBERING DETAILS

2. The Mbanta villagers decided to shun the Christians because

(A) the Christians destroyed the gods of their ancestors.

(B) they thought a Christian killed a sacred python.

(C) the poor crops showed that the gods were displeased.

(D) too many of the villagers' sons had joined the new religion and were ignoring their ancestors.

DRAWING CONCLUSIONS

3. Okonkwo hosted an especially huge feast before he left Mbanta because

(A) he wanted to show what a great man he was.

(B) he had promised Uchendu he would host a great feast.

(C) he wanted word of his generosity to travel back to Umuofia.

(D) he knew he owed it to his mother's village.

IDENTIFYING THE MOOD

4. When the *osu* first entered the Christian church, those worshipping were

(A) pleased to have new converts.

(B) disturbed that outcasts felt they could attend.

(C) eager to show the outcasts that they were welcome.

(D) gloomy that the only converts they could get were outcasts.

CRITICAL THINKING

5. **Summarize** Describe why Nwoye came to study at the white man's school in Umuofia.

6. **Comprehension** Explain why the elders decided to give the Christians land in the Evil Forest for their church.

7. **Analysis** Explain why you think the *osu* became the strongest members of the new church.

CHAPTERS 20–25

FINDING THE MAIN IDEA

1. Chapters 20–25 are mainly about

(A) how Okonkwo struggled to regain his place in Umuofia.

(B) the conflict between the Africans and the white men.

(C) the gradual conversion of all the people of Umuofia into the new church.

(D) how the white men began with their church and then brought a government, as well.

REMEMBERING DETAILS

2. Why is Okonkwo unable to initiate his sons into the *ozo* society as he had planned?

(A) His sons are not interested.

(B) He does not have enough money to do it.

(C) The church has outlawed all titles in the clan.

(D) The ceremony is only performed once every three years.

DRAWING CONCLUSIONS

3. Okonkwo's extreme reaction after the arrival of the missionaries is because

(A) he wants to provoke his fellow villagers to go to war.

(B) he is not able to adapt to the new ways.

(C) the missionaries would not allow him to stay in Umuofia.

(D) his sons have left him.

IDENTIFYING THE MOOD

4. As they return to the village, the imprisoned men are

(A) angry.

(B) ashamed.

(C) resigned.

(D) both A and B.

CRITICAL THINKING

5. **Compare and Contrast** Explain the differences and similarities between Mr. Brown and Mr. Smith.

6. **Comprehension** Explain the District Commissioner's thought in the last paragraph of the book.

7. **Analysis** Explain what the author was trying to convey to readers in the last paragraph of the book.